Advance Praise for

How to Be a Business Superhero

"Wise combines commerce with capes, sales with spandex, and marketing with mutants. If you want to see business with Superman's X-ray vision clarity, read this book."

—Don Tapscott, coauthor of
the bestseller *Wikinomics*

"Captain America teaches leadership; Spider-Man, responsibility; Batman, the power of preparation. Wise's book will entertain, inform, and inspire you . . . even if you don't wear a cape or cowl."

—Leonard Brody, CEO of NowPublic and
author of *Innovation Nation*

"Who would have thought the cape-and-cowl community had so much to teach the suit-and-tie crowd? Anyone seeking a novel, inspirational, entertaining read need look no further."

—Jeff Howe, contributing editor,
Wired magazine

HOW TO BE A BUSINESS SUPERHERO

PREPARE FOR EVERYTHING

TRAIN WITH THE BEST

MAKE YOUR OWN DESTINY AT WORK

SEAN WISE, BA, LLB, MBA

A PERIGEE BOOK

A PERIGEE BOOK
Published by the Penguin Group
Penguin Group (USA) Inc.
375 Hudson Street, New York, New York 10014, USA
Penguin Group (Canada), 90 Eglinton Avenue East, Suite 700, Toronto, Ontario M4P 2Y3, Canada
(a division of Pearson Penguin Canada Inc.)
Penguin Books Ltd., 80 Strand, London WC2R 0RL, England
Penguin Group Ireland, 25 St. Stephen's Green, Dublin 2, Ireland (a division of Penguin Books Ltd.)
Penguin Group (Australia), 250 Camberwell Road, Camberwell, Victoria 3124, Australia
(a division of Pearson Australia Group Pty. Ltd.)
Penguin Books India Pvt. Ltd., 11 Community Centre, Panchsheel Park, New Delhi—110 017, India
Penguin Group (NZ), 67 Apollo Drive, Rosedale, North Shore 0632, New Zealand
(a division of Pearson New Zealand Ltd.)
Penguin Books (South Africa) (Pty.) Ltd., 24 Sturdee Avenue, Rosebank, Johannesburg 2196,
South Africa

Penguin Books Ltd., Registered Offices: 80 Strand, London WC2R 0RL, England

Interior illustrations by Paul Gilligan
Cover art by Paul Gilligan
Text design by Ellen Cipriano

First edition: September 2008

Library of Congress Cataloging-in-Publication Data

Wise, Sean.
How to be a business superhero : prepare for everything, train with the best, make your own destiny at work / Sean Wise.
p. cm.
Includes index.
ISBN 978-0-399-53456-0
1. Career development. 2. Mentoring in business. 3. Role models. 4. Success in business.
I. Title.
HF5381.W773 2008
650.1—dc22 2008021586

PRINTED IN THE UNITED STATES OF AMERICA

10 9 8 7 6 5 4 3 2 1

To my fiancée, Allie Hughes,
Who makes me feel like a superhero
Each and every day

CONTENTS

Introduction xi

PART I **SUPERHEROES 101** **1**

1. The Ten Golden Rules 3

PART II **LESSONS FROM THE LEGENDS** **39**

2. Batman: Preparation Leads to Success 41
3. The Green Lantern: The Will and the Way 47
4. Deadman: Gain Perspective 57
5. Spawn: Think Before You Act 61
6. Superman: Know Your Weakness 66
7. Robin: Learn from Others 71
8. Captain Marvel: SWIPE Often 75

9. Thor: Look for Opportunities 84
10. Hellboy: Create Your Destiny 88
11. The Silver Surfer: Outwit Ultimatums 92
12. The Hulk: Keep Your Cool 97
13. Wonder Woman: Stay Focused 101
14. Black Bolt: Silence Is Golden 106
15. Wolverine: Strive for Excellence 113
16. Iron Man: The Need for Continuous Improvement 117
17. Spider-Man: With Great Power Comes Great Responsibility 122
18. Madrox: Synergistic Multitasking 130
19. Justice League: Even Superheroes Need Help 134
20. Green Arrow: Target a Niche 139
21. Captain America: Leadership Best Practices 143
22. Oracle: Build a Network 149
23. Doctor Strange: Never Too Late to Change 153
24. Mr. Fantastic: Be Flexible 156
25. Fantastic Four: It Takes All Types 159
26. Plastic Man: Have Fun 165
27. The Legion of Super-Heroes: The Power of Diversity 169
28. Midnighter: Play the Movie in Advance 174

PART III **BRING ON THE BAD GUYS** 181

29. Dr. Doom: Avoid Enlightened Despotism 183
30. Sinestro: Choose Inspiration over Fear 188
31. Magneto: Avoid Zealotry 196
32. Lex Luthor: Ego Check 200
33. The Joker: Too Far out of the Box 206
34. Mystique: Be Yourself 210
35. Catwoman: Perspective Matters 214

APPENDICES 221

The Business Superhero Mnemonic 221
The Ten Golden Rules for All Aspiring Superheroes 223
Business Superhero Lessons Learned 225
Comic Books 101 231

Index 237

INTRODUCTION

Some idolize athletes, others movie stars. For me it was, it is, and it will always be superheroes. Whom we choose as our heroes says a lot about us. After all, our heroes are the figures that we wish to become. The people we seek to emulate. Those we secretly fantasize about being—in those moments when we allow our imaginations to drift into a realm of enhanced possibility. So if that is true, what does my admiration of the cape and cowl set say about me?

I was born in the 1970s and grew up during the tail end of the cold war. The world at that time was becoming grayer by the day. Good and Bad were becoming less clear as the baby boomers were struggling to find their moral compass. It was during that time that I first met and fell in love with superheroes.

I read my first superhero comic (*Justice League of America* #133) in 1982, at the age of twelve. It was the first part of a two-parter guest starring Supergirl, so once I finished it I just had to go out and get the next issue. From that point on, I was hooked.

WHY DO SUPERHEROES MAKE GOOD ROLE MODELS?

Even today, in an era of adult comics that star darker heroes doing darker things, superheroes are still the role models I'd want my kids (should I ever be blessed with some) to look up to. For me, heroes provide the basis for a moral compass. They provide readers with modern-day parables that espouse core values, including but not limited to:

* The ability to overcome adversity, to see the good guys triumph over tragedy
* The idea that being different is a characteristic to be embraced
* The clear sense of right and wrong that commits one to protecting the innocent and defending the underdog

These three themes run through the stories of all true superheroes. Let's look at the themes individually.

Overcoming Adversity

Batman, Superman, Spider-Man—they have lots in common, most notably the fact that each character is formed as a result of the death of parental figures. The death of Bruce Wayne's parents at the hands of mugger Joe Chill inspires Bruce to dedicate his life to justice. Superman is the sole survivor of Krypton and finds himself an orphaned stranger in a strange land. Spider-Man learns that "with great power comes great responsibility" only after his selfish decisions lead to the death of his uncle Ben.

The theme of turning tragedy into triumph is central to most superheroes and helps teach us that, although circumstances may be beyond our control, the actions we take as a result *are* in our control. Therefore, it is up to us to decide if we will allow our hardships to diminish or strengthen us.

Daring to Be Different

I remember reading *The X-Men* during Chris Claremont's legendary stint writing this group of antiheroes. One of the central themes of Claremont's sixteen-year run was that the X-Men were the ultimate minority. Born mutants (beings with powers that set them apart), they were tasked with "defending those who fear them." This irony allowed Claremont to explore both race relations and the treatment of minorities, but it also provided his teenage readers an arena in which to contemplate their own experiences of alienation. After all, most teenagers feel at one point or another that they, like the X-Men, are outsiders who live in a world that respects neither their uniqueness nor their point of view.

In exploring this theme and compelling his readers to do the same, Claremont illustrated the second recurring theme in superhero comics—tolerance of differences—in a way that permits us to embrace individuality.

Superheroes often encourage us to dare to be different by their example. After all, if the protagonists valued homogeneity and conformity, would they ever don their garish costumes in the first place?

Defending the Underdog

The X-Men saw themselves as protectors. They protected humans from evil mutants, they protected mutants from human prejudice, and they even protected the people of Earth from invading alien hordes. *Defending the weak* is a recurring theme for superheroes of all shapes and sizes. By standing unashamedly for "Truth, Justice and the American Way," Superman actually helped define what the "American way" was. Almost to a fault, superheroes impose their moral compass on others, defending the weak against those who exploit their powers and abilities for evil. In so doing, they help define what is and is not acceptable. One of comic's greatest examples of this is Spider-Man.

The story of Spider-Man's origin typically ends with the maxim: With great power comes great responsibility. Some claim that Spidey's creator, the legendary Stan Lee, borrowed this axiom from Winston Churchill's 1946 address to President Harry S Truman, while others attribute the origins of the saying to the

French *noblesse oblige* (which means literally "nobility obligates" but means figuratively "social responsibility necessarily attends wealth, prestige, or power"). Regardless of the original source for such maxims, one thing is certain: Superheroes teach readers of all ages the importance of overcoming adversity, defending the weak, and ensuring that justice prevails. And *that's* why superheroes are my role models.

BEING HEROIC

All superheroes share several characteristics. Adjectives that describe all superheroes (including Business Superheroes) are honorable, extraordinary, relentless, outspoken, inspirational, and courageous. Collectively, these words form the acronym *HEROIC.*

***H* is for honorable.** Heroes stick to a self-imposed moral code—a code that commits them to do the right thing, regardless of personal sacrifice.

***E* is for extraordinary.** Heroes aren't afraid to stand out. In fact, they often pursue courses of action (like wearing a costume or standing up for what's right when others demur) that highlight just how distinctive and extraordinary they are.

***R* is for relentless.** Being a superhero takes dedication. Heroes are constantly training, constantly striving to improve.

***O* is for outspoken.** Being a superhero means standing up for what you believe in and not going with the flow when you know the flow is wrong.

***I* is for inspirational.** Heroes do more than simply right wrongs—they inspire others to follow their example and bring out the heroic qualities in those around them.

***C* is for courageous.** Speaking out against injustice, inspiring others, being extraordinary—these things all require courage, the courage to be different, to overcome fear, and to triumph over tragedy.

WHAT THE #@$% IS A BUSINESS SUPERHERO?

A Business Superhero is nothing more than a person in business who strives for greatness—strives to be extraordinary. Someone who dares to dream about changing the world through a personal dedication to success rather than being satisfied simply to arrive at work, punch in, go through the motions, and punch out.

Dale Carnegie, Bill Gates, Jack Welch, and Sir Richard Branson all qualify as Business Superheroes (for more on these men, see Part II) because each one fits the HEROIC standard. So you see, superheroes can be found in places other than comic book stores. Applying the HEROIC standard to our conduct in the business arena only further illustrates this point:

***H* is for honorable.** Some businesspeople take as their mantra: It's not personal, it's only business. And although business decisions should be made when one is unclouded by sentimentality, this idea should not be used by executives to rationalize inappropriate actions. Cutting corners, breaking your word, or acting in some other dishonorable manner may sometimes seem necessary or even commonplace in the business world. But in my experience, such an unheroic action tends to generate only short-term gains at the cost of long-term pain. Business Superheroes maintain integrity at all times. Katherine Graham offers proof that this is in fact possible for a successful businessperson. Graham, the former publisher of the *Washington Post* and a Business Superhero known for personal integrity, would constantly ask her journalists and herself, Did we get it right? Was the story fair? Could we have done it better?

***E* is for extraordinary.** Business Superheroes choose to be extraordinary. They choose to give 110 percent, to be on time each and every time, and to underpromise and overdeliver. Most of all, they choose to go beyond what is usual, regular, or customary.

***R* is for relentless.** Time and time again, you hear business innovators tell you, in the words of Thomas Alva Edison, "Success is 10 percent inspiration and 90 percent perspiration." All good things take work and heroes know that. A hero never gives up. You can beat her to the ground, burn down her secret lair, mesmerize her with hypnotic rays, and even send an army of killer toys after her. But in the end, the true hero perseveres and relentlessly pursues her goals. No matter the personal cost.

***O* is for outspoken.** Heroes aren't afraid to stand out. The same is true of business superstars. True high achievers stand up to be counted, volunteer for the tough assignments that nobody else wants, and—most of all—let their presence be known.

***I* is for inspirational.** Business leaders know that to lead, they must inspire others. After all, why wear a distinctive, brightly colored costume if you don't want to attract attention? But attention isn't enough, the right kind of attention is key. The world of superheroes is a modern-day mythology and, like the mythical figures of old, most heroes have at their core a parable or lesson to teach. Some do it explicitly through example, others through inspiration, but regardless of the method the message is the same: Do good, fight injustice, and keep the faith.

***C* is for courageous.** Success requires risk. Michael Eisner, the former CEO of Disney, put it best in his interview with the Academy of Achievement: "When you're trying to create things that are new, you have to be prepared to be on the edge of risk." Risk takes

> courage—courage to go against the grain, courage to innovate, courage to do the right thing.

So, throughout this book, when you read the term *Business Superhero* conjure up your own personal business heroes, be they Jack Welch and Donald Trump, Oprah Winfrey and Mary Kay Ash, Michael Eisner and Bill Gates, or Lee Iacocca and Lou Gerstner. Just imagine your hero in a cape.

WHY BE A BUSINESS SUPERHERO?

Would you rather be Batman or Alfred the Butler? Would you rather be Wonder Woman or Col. Steve Trevor? Superman or Lois Lane? Being a Business Superhero isn't just a concept; it is a way of life. It's something to aspire to. And the world needs more superheroes of all kinds—including and especially in business—now maybe more than ever.

Much like the Dark Age of Comics, which was an arduous time for comic superheroes (see "Comic Book History 101"), the last twenty years have not been a good time for business heroes. Enron, Worldcom, and other scandalized corporations stole the dreams and futures of hundreds of thousands of innocent, hard-working people, all to line the pockets of a handful of Business Supervillains. Lay, Black, Keating, Stewart, and Milken have joined the ranks of their comic book counterparts, to show us that power can corrupt if not wedded to integrity and principled behavior.

Similarly, our faith in those who have traditionally served as role models in our society has suffered greatly over the last decade. Barry Bonds shattered the hearts of those who looked up to him and other sports figures. He and a host of other disgraced athletes have shown us (as comics do) that, for some people, the ends of fame and wealth will always justify the means. The falls from grace of Paris, Britney, Michael Jackson, and all of their tabloid brethren have certainly dissipated any hope of relying on entertainers to serve as role models.

But there is light on the horizon. With the start of the Modern Age of Comics (see "Comic Book History 101"), we are seeing a diminished presence of the dark, flawed antiheroes who pervaded the Dark Age and a renaissance of the more overtly heroic role models from the classic ages of comics. Business may be promoting a similar change of character type.

Warren Buffet in 2006 announced a plan to give his fortune to charity—his donation will amount to over $30 billion. Bill Gates has now given up his emperor's throne to devote his ingenuity, wealth, and celebrity to find solutions to the AIDS crisis in Africa. Al Gore, now a venture capitalist in Silicon Valley, is fighting global warming one investment at a time. Since 2006, award-winning author Shel Horowitz has been leading a campaign to get 25,000 business leaders from around the globe to sign a business ethics pledge, committing them not only to run their business ethically but also to recruit 100 other businesspeople to sign on. Even large multinational conglomerates are making efforts to improve their practices.

Throughout the nation and the world, heroes are rising up in business. The real question is, Do you want to join their ranks?

If . . .

- ★ All you want is a paycheck
- ★ You are satisfied punching the clock
- ★ You prefer your choices to be dictated by convenience rather than by conviction
- ★ You are content to stay unknown

. . . then this book isn't for you.

But if . . .

- ★ You want to be the best that you can be
- ★ You want your dedication to success and integrity to shape two-thirds of your waking hours (which is often how much time we spend at work)
- ★ You want to leave the world a better place than you found it

. . . then you want to be a Business Superhero.

HOW TO USE THIS BOOK

This book is divided into three distinct but interrelated sections.

Part I: "Superheroes 101," in which I explain the basics of becoming a Business Superhero
Part II: "Lessons from the Legends," in which specific superheroes teach us how to be Business Superheroes
Part III: "Bring on the Bad Guys," in which I examine cautionary tales of superpowers gone bad and analyze what supervillains can teach us

My hope is that you will read this book with a pen in hand and so become an active reader—whether you're underlining key points or doodling your thoughts in the margin. That pen will also help when you come to the exercises that I invite you to do throughout the book. Take the time to complete them—I hope they inspire you.

I have also created a website for your use (www.BusinessSuperheroes.com). There you can use the HeroMachine to create your virtual costume, find links to help you create a superhero business card, and information to keep you up-to-date on forthcoming lectures related to Business Superheroes. Enjoy the book; I hope to get the chance to discuss it with you online.

Onwards and Upwards!
Sean Wise

PART I

SUPERHEROES 101

In this section, I lay down the Ten Golden Rules that should be the starting point for every Business Superhero. I discuss:

* How a work/life balance is part of establishing your MO
* How patrolling networking events can serve you in the long run
* How team-ups with other heroes can help you overcome almost any hazard

THE TEN GOLDEN RULES

By this point, I hope you have decided that your destiny lies in becoming a Business Superhero. Good for you—the world needs more Business Superheroes. So what comes next? Expose yourself to gamma radiation? Hang out in labs, hoping to get bitten by a radioactive spider? Watch the night skies for alien ships? I'm happy to tell you nothing that strange is required. To be a Business Superhero, you simply have to decide to be one and then follow the Ten Golden Rules for all superheroes.

GOLDEN RULE 1: DO NO EVIL

In Oliver Stone's classic 1987 film *Wall Street*, billionaire corporate raider Gordon Gekko (played by Michael Douglas) espouses the virtues of greed. Specifically, the seminal icon of the 1980s states: "[G]reed, for lack of a better word, is good. Greed is right, greed works. Greed clarifies, cuts through, and captures the

The Ten Golden Rules for All Aspiring Superheroes	
1. Do no evil	*Karma's the worst supervillain*
2. Swear an oath	*The purpose-driven hero*
3. Establish your MO	*Work/life balance*
4. Craft an identity	*Building Brand You*
5. Keep your secrets	*Confidentiality at work*
6. Establish a hideout	*Everyone needs a Batcave*
7. Keep odd hours	*Early rise, early wise*
8. Be ready for team-ups	*1 + 1 = more, in the hero business*
9. Patrol often	*Network, network, network*
10. Overcome adversity	*Overcoming obstacles*

essence of the evolutionary spirit. Greed, in all of its forms; greed for life, for money, for love, knowledge has marked the upward surge of mankind."

Greed is good is actually painted on the wall of my office. But you have to read the whole quote to understand Gekko's true meaning.

First, *greed* here refers to the desired pursuit of something (anything); it is the spirit that drives you to acquire more (money, information, success) than you currently have. Second, Gekko depicts greed as aspiration in action; it is the essence of the evolutionary spirit and of progress. It is only when greed forces you to do evil things (as it does to Gekko) that it becomes a problem.

This illustrates a fundamental lesson that Business Superheroes should learn early on: Like greed, goals are for the most part neither good nor evil—it is the means you employ to pursue your goals that render your actions praiseworthy or blameworthy.

Is it wrong to want a big salary?	Not if you aim to acquire it honorably
Is it wrong to want to succeed?	Not if you can do so without harming others
Is it wrong to negotiate a good deal?	Not unless you use unethical means to do so

The quest for and acquisition of wealth are not considered vices in comic books. After all, many superheroes are millionaires in their civilian identities. In fact, in 2007, *Forbes* identified Bruce Wayne (aka Batman) as the eighth-richest fictional character, with personal holdings worth approximately $6.5 billion. Contrast Bruce with Lex Luthor (Superman's arch-nemesis and fourth in the 2005 *Forbes* list): Both are billionaire industrialists, both service the U.S. military, both have undertaken corporate raids; yet only one's actions are painted as evil. Why? Because, as in so many things, it is the means—not the ends—that define the actions.

For those reasons, Business Superheroes should follow the credo of another entrepreneur who left a powerful legacy to humanity—William Shakespeare, who wrote in *All's Well That Ends Well*: "Love all, trust a few, / Do wrong to none" (act I, scene 1).

Still not convinced that this is a credo for a Business Superhero? Well, let's take another perspective: karma. From a layperson's perspective, karma is interpreted to mean:

- ★ What goes around comes around.
- ★ Don't do the crime if you can't do the time.
- ★ If you do bad things to others, expect bad things to happen to you.

Basically, if you screw over others in business, then expect to be screwed over yourself. It is an unfortunate fact of business that you may always get screwed over by unethical people, regardless of whether you have merited it karmically or not. However, my firsthand experience tells me that unethical treatment of others makes the prospect of being treated unethically a virtual certainty (for more, see Chapter 5).

Regardless of whether you "Do no evil" out of altruism or simply because you fear repercussions, I recommend that you keep this principle foremost in your mind as you evolve into a Business Superhero.

GOLDEN RULE 2: SWEAR AN OATH

Oaths are stated commitments. When superheroes recite an oath, they are reinforcing their promise to commit to a specific action and/or pattern of behavior. Most superheroes swear an oath. The most famous is the oath taken by the Green Lantern each time he recharges his power ring (see Chapter 3):

In brightest day; In blackest night.
No Evil shall escape my sight. Let those who worship's Evil's might,
Beware my power. . . . Green Lantern's Light!

Here are two others:

- ⋆ **The Phantom.** I swear to devote my life to the destruction of piracy, greed, cruelty, and injustice!
- ⋆ **Batman.** I swear to dedicate my life and my inheritance to bringing your murderer, and all criminals, to justice. I swear it.

The Business Superhero Oath

One of my favorite books is *The Monk Who Sold His Ferrari*, by Robin Sharma, who also wrote *The Greatness Guide*. In both texts, Sharma discusses the meaning of life, stating, "The purpose of life is a life of purpose." Sharma's message is as simple as it sounds: If you want to have meaning in your life, do things that are meaningful.

Billy Crystal's character, Mitch, in the 1991 comedy *City Slickers* discovers this same parable when talking to Jack Palance's character, Curly:

CURLY: You know what the secret of life is? [*Holds up one finger.*] This.

MITCH: Your finger?

CURLY: One thing. Just one thing. You stick to that and everything else don't mean shit.

MITCH: But, what's the "one thing"?

CURLY: [*Smiles.*] That's what *you* have to find out.

The one thing that makes life worth living is a very personal and specific thing, and the quest to discover that thing is worthy of superheroes and mere mortals alike. People usually discover their one thing in solitude and reflection and often keep it private. But superheroes—including Business Superheroes—don't have that luxury. They need to decide their one thing, declare it openly, and pursue it relentlessly.

Why Business Superheroes Need an Oath

In addition to helping you focus on your goals and values, a Business Superhero oath—or personal mission statement—helps you communicate your value and values to others. My own mission statement is, "Wise counsel for smart companies." Not only does this reaffirm my selected purpose in life (that is, adding value) but it also conveys my goals to others simply and powerfully. My mission statement appears on all my cards, websites, and promotional material.

Crafting Your Oath

Much like creating your own personal brand (see Golden Rule 4: Building Brand You), a personal mission statement is critical to becoming a Business Superhero. So what is your oath?

For companies, a business oath often takes the form of what is commonly called "an elevator pitch." This term comes from the urban myth about an entrepreneur who, seeking capital, followed an investor into an elevator in the latter's office tower. The entrepreneur then had only the time it took the elevator to go from the lobby to the penthouse (where the investor's offices were located) to pitch his deal. Success resulted in an invitation into the investor's boardroom for a more formal pitch. (Failure would result in an unceremonious call to the security desk.)

The Elevator Pitch

The elevator pitch (or business oath) is a two-minute oath that tells listeners what problem the business will solve and how.

SUPERHERO EXERCISE 1

Crafting an Oath

Here are three questions to help you create your own oath:

- ★What would I like to be remembered for? (Honesty? Creativity? Success?)
- ★Who is it I wish to serve? (A community? An industry? A company?)
- ★How can I say it succinctly?

Once you have your oath, write it on a sticky note and put it on your bathroom mirror. Every morning as you brush your teeth, repeat your mission statement (that is, swear your oath). Then be vigilant throughout the day for opportunities to make good on your oath. Do this for a month, and you will be amazed at the results.

Consultants call this the "mission statement." An indispensable piece of branding, the mission statement serves to distill the essence of what makes a company or product unique by indicating its role and value. In my business—venture capital—my colleagues and I hear five to six elevator pitches a day; and yes, those two-minute pitches often significantly shape our decisions about which opportunities we will pursue.

A strong elevator pitch alone will not get you a check from me, but a bad elevator pitch will almost certainly kill your chances. Thus an effective, short statement is necessary but not sufficient for raising capital. But an elevator pitch is important for more than just selling your deal to investors: A good business oath shows others that management has a clear vision for the company and can articulate it in a concise and convincing manner.

Elevator pitches are also important for the Business Superheroes who run these enterprises. As I discuss later (see Golden Rule 4: Building Brand You), today's free-agent economy requires that people—not just ventures—be able to articulate their value concisely and consistently, and increasingly this must be accomplished by crafting an elevator pitch.

A good elevator pitch is made up of two distinct parts: A pain statement and a value proposition. The pain statement refers to the problem you can solve, and the value proposition illustrates how you solve that problem.

Let's look at two fictional elevator pitches to illustrate this point:

- One person's trash is another's treasure (pain statement). Our global online garage sale brings together buyers and sellers, facilitating the efficient movement of goods from one person's trash pile to another's treasure chest (value proposition).
- People want to have sex longer than their bodies will allow (pain statement). Our blue, aspirin-size, FDA-approved tablet allows them to do so in a highly non-invasive manner (value proposition).

The first is my made-up elevator pitch for eBay; the second, for Viagra. Each qualifies as a solid elevator pitch for a business because each meets the following four criteria:

Concise	Keep it under two minutes.
Irrefutable	Stick to indisputable, objective facts. (For example, would anyone really dispute that "people want to have sex longer than their bodies allow"?)
Greed inducing	Inspire passion by getting the listener excited about the opportunity and its potential value.
Easy to understand	Avoid technical terms, ensuring that even your grandma and grandkids can get it. (Note that I never mentioned the chemical composition of the pill because that would be lost on most people.)

Now you see that every Business Superhero needs an elevator pitch. Superman stands for "Truth, Justice, and the American

Way," the Green Lantern vows that "No evil shall escape my sight." So what's your elevator pitch? Mine is:

> Growing billion-dollar businesses by bridging the gap between entrepreneurs and equity, Wise Mentor Capital provides wise counsel to smart companies.

And my personal mission statement is:

> Being an entrepreneur is the 3rd-toughest job in the world.* Sean Wise adds value to entrepreneurs by sharing best practices, facilitating access to congruent capital and leveraging networked communities of knowledge.

GOLDEN RULE 3: ESTABLISH YOUR MO

Okay, so now that we have agreed to do no evil and have sworn our oaths, it is on to the next step, creating an MO, or modus operandi—Latin for "mode of operation," which is fancy talk for "way of doing things." Spidey swings through Manhattan, his spider-sense alerting him to danger. Batman responds to a spotlight shining in the night sky. Hellboy works for the Bureau for Paranormal Research and Defense, which is tasked with defending humanity from "things that go bump in the night." So what will be your MO?

*The toughest two being parent and spouse, respectively.

When trying to decide how you will fulfill your oath (see Golden Rule 2: Swear an oath), you need to consider how much of yourself (your time, your focus, your money) you are willing to commit. This is a highly personal decision, but one that crafting an oath should make easier because it helps you clarify your priorities. From a business perspective, deciding on your work/life balance (that is, how much time you will spend daily on business matters) correlates to the question that most comic book heroes face early in their careers: Whether or not to maintain a secret identity. Characters like Hellboy and Aquaman have private lives but no real secret identities. They are their "hero selves" all the time. Now, that doesn't mean they lack downtime or opportunities to relax; it just means they do so as Hellboy and Aquaman, respectively. In this respect they are unlike Superman and Batman, who choose to maintain identities that are distinct from their superhero ones.

As you begin to craft your identity, decide if you want to keep your work and personal lives separate or together. Neither strategy is correct; each offers its own MO.

MO 1: Secret identity. Maintain a dual identity by separating your business life from your personal life. This means that you rarely socialize with your work colleagues and that you are largely off-duty when you go home. This is the approach most people take, and it can work well if you don't need to be "on" 24/7.

MO 2: Public identity. Some people find it too difficult to maintain two distinct worlds and prefer a more

> integrated approach. I discuss the use of synergistic multitasking later (see Chapter 18), but for now, the public identity route is one more often associated with Business Superheroes like Donald Trump and Gene Simmons. The Donald is never *not* The Donald. Similarly, if you have ever watched his show *Family Jewels*, you have probably recognized that Simmons has no Off switch.

Again, neither is right or wrong, although the latter tends to be the approach of the majority of Business Superheroes profiled throughout this book, if only because their public identities have served to make them more recognizable, accessible examples. In the end, it all depends on how you define *quality of life*. I love what I do, and so it's not work to me, it's just how I live my life—Blackberry in one hand, and coffee in the other.

GOLDEN RULE 4: CRAFT AN IDENTITY

One of the biggest changes to business over the last few years is the rise of what author Don Pink calls the "free-agent nation," in his book of the same name. This concept refers to the growing workforce trend in which key members of teams are increasingly understood to be contractors, free to move from company to company, rather than employees, who are locked into one company for a lifetime. This trend coincides with the rise of the theory of "Brand

You" (that is, you are the brand), which maintains that, like products and companies, people can stand for ideals and market themselves accordingly. These two concepts are connected: Because workers have professional mobility, employers have a choice when hiring contractors, and just as the public buys from companies based on brand, employers are starting to do the same.

Almost all superheroes are brands onto themselves. Batman conjures up the image of intense, brooding dedication to fighting crime. Superman conjures up the ideals of Truth, Justice and the American Way. The Hulk conjures up images of powerful green rage. So what is your brand?

SUPERHERO EXERCISE 2

Start with What Really Matters

Before deciding on your brand, first decide what matters most to you. Fetch a blank piece of paper and undertake this exercise:

> Imagine that it is fifty years hence. You are dead and watching your own funeral. Now write down words that you hope will be used in your eulogy.

Will you be described as dedicated? Honest? Reliable? Creative? A team player? A leader? Don't ask yourself what others would say today, ask yourself what you *hope* they will be saying when you are no longer around. These words are the foundation of Brand You because they represent the traits that you treasure the most—your highest personal ideals. They should, in turn, shape your priorities, so that your actions continually reflect and affirm what's really important to you. By committing yourself to realizing these values you adopt a life of purpose, making these traits essential to your Business Superhero identity.

In his 1999 classic, *The Brand You50*, Tom Peters—who is often named the most influential management theorist of the modern age by the likes of *Forbes*, *Fortune*, and *Fast Company*—waxes extensively on the fact that white collar workers now face the same outsourcing that eliminated so many manufacturing positions over the last two decades. In his article "The Brand Called You" (from the August 1997 issue of *Fast Company*), Peters emphatically encourages today's knowledge workers to create a distinct persona for their business identity. A persona that will set you apart from others, a persona that will convey your value to others, and most of all a persona that will allow you to be seen as necessary and distinct.

Consistency—The Key to Brand You

Regardless of the attributes you wish to assimilate into Brand You, the key is consistency. After all, you don't expect Batman to be wearing fluorescent pink, just as you don't expect Superman to be stealing candy from a baby. Consistency is one of the keys in business. By consciously shaping the impressions you make, you are more likely to mold those impressions into a brand. You need to ensure that your actions consistently match the brand that you cultivate. After all, you can't build a brand based on reliability and then be late regularly.

Clothes Make the Hero

I've been a lawyer, a corporate finance agent, a public speaker, a professor, and a venture capitalist. Each of these professions has its own dress code. More important, what I wore was often the basis of people's first impressions.

The dress code for lawyers is a suit and tie, but it was up to me to decide to wear a perfectly pressed high-end suit or a wrinkled off-the-rack suit. Either way, my brand would be affected by my costume. The same is true for all Business Superheroes. It

SUPERHERO EXERCISE 3

Crafting a Costume

Before walking too far on the road to Business Superherodom, you will need to craft your costume. Ask yourself these questions:

1. How do I want to be perceived? Do I want to look conservative or cutting edge?
2. With whom will I be dealing on a daily basis? Are they my clients or am I their client? Do I have a boss or am I the boss?
3. How do successful people in my field dress?
4. What is the standard dress at my workplace?
5. How might my appearance be able to reflect what is unique about my value or brand?

Based on the answers to these questions, you can begin to craft a costume that befits your new Business Superhero identity.

may not be fair, but people judge you by the clothes you wear. Accept this fact of life and use it to your advantage by making a conscious choice to adopt an appearance that matches the brand you are trying to establish.

GOLDEN RULE 5: KEEP YOUR SECRETS

When I first became a manager, a lot changed for me. By far the greatest change was my relationship with my peers, some of

whom now reported to me. Later in the book, I discuss the difference between a manager and a leader as well as the difference between positional power (power derived from a title or role) and personal power (power derived from qualities, regardless of rank or title). While I had always been a leader with personal power (that's how I got promoted in the first place), I had never been a manager with positional power.

One of the adjustments I had to make was in the level of disclosure I had with my team. Before taking the role, I had shared the ups and downs of both my personal and business life with my peers, but after being promoted I learned a lesson that Wess Roberts and Bill Ross teach in *Make It So: Leadership Lessons from Star Trek, The Next Generation*—While the crew is free to share with the captain, the reverse is never true. Consequently, I needed to strengthen communications upward (so that I was always in the loop), but I never again shared personal information downward. If my team was worried about revenue, I wanted them to raise their concerns with me; but if I was worried about revenue, sharing my concerns could have undermined my team's confidence or, worse yet, led to reactions that could compromise our effectiveness as a team by hurting morale or distracting the members from our collective task.

For those reasons, I suggest all Business Superheroes establish a one-way communications policy—that is, don't share your secrets with juniors. After all, sharing your burden in the short term only hurts you in the long term since a burden shared is rarely a burden lessened, at least in business. Sharing your knowledge that someone is soon to be fired neither affects the outcome nor makes that outcome any easier. All that it stands to do is magnify the possibility that the information will spread further, and thus create a scenario that risks humiliating the individual involved and disrupting general morale.

Another example—one that pains me to discuss—is that of misbehavior at Christmas parties. I once worked at a multinational accounting firm that (in my day) was known for having a Christmas party like no other. They hired rock bands, rented massive convention centers, and invited 5,000 of their closest friends to attend. Regardless of the fact that these events were most definitely business functions, not a year would go by without someone consuming too much alcohol and doing something inappropriate. One year it was a staff member who seemed to lose his pants near the end of the night. Shocking indeed, but no less shocking was the behavior of a senior partner at the next year's party. Like the staff member before him, this partner had enjoyed liberal use of the free bar. Although there is nothing wrong with that per se, I did find it offensive when he proceeded to inappropriately fondle female attendees at the event, including my girlfriend and the life partners of several of his peers.

Of course, while the actions of both the senior partner and the junior associate were clearly inappropriate, one was held to a much higher standard—the standard that comes with leadership. In all the years since, I have maintained a strict policy concerning where and when I let my guard down. Listen, I'm not a prude—far from it; I've been known to consume a beer or two in my life. But after seeing the effects of my colleagues' actions, I quickly chose to let my guard down with only my friends and family, not my work colleagues.

So if you plan on being a Business Superhero, you may want to heed this advice and protect your secret identity by keeping your personal and business lives separate, just as Kal-el keeps his identity of Clark Kent separate from his Superman persona.

GOLDEN RULE 6: ESTABLISH A HIDEOUT

Everyone needs a place to call his or her own. The Fantastic Four have the Baxter Building; Batman has the Batcave; and, of course, there is always Superman's Fortress of Solitude. Superheroes typ-

Superman's Fortress of Solitude, which first appeared in June 1958 in *Action Comics* #254, was actually based on Doc Savage's arctic headquarters (also known as the Fortress of Solitude), first mentioned in the 1933 pulp novel *Man of Bronze*.

ically create a hideout to gain privacy, to have a place to think without distraction, and—most of all—to have a safe place to decompress after tough battles.

Similarly, Business Superheroes need somewhere to wind down. It could be a conference room on a floor other than yours, a coffee shop down the street, or even a mountain cabin. I recommend picking at least two spots:

- ★ A safe haven for shedding the day-to-day stuff. For example, I start every day at Starbucks. There, I make my to-do list, get caught up on email, and decide where my focus for the day should lie.
- ★ A Fortress of Solitude for escaping the larger, longer-term stuff. Whenever I need to plan strategy, set life goals, or reconsider an approach I've been taking, I retreat to my cottage by the lake. There, the distance from the office and the absence of distraction permit me to clear my head, reevaluate my priorities, and recharge my spirit.

GOLDEN RULE 7: KEEP ODD HOURS

How tired must Batman be? Up all night thwarting evil, then home only long enough to exchange his bat-costume for a suit and tie, before going to work all day as CEO of Wayne Enterprises. Then home again to change into his tuxedo before going out to dinner, in his billionaire playboy persona. Then back to fighting crime, often before dessert. Now that's got to be one heck of a tiring lifestyle, but it's the price one pays for being a superhero.

Business Superheroes the world over pay a similar price. Benjamin Franklin (who was an avid inventor and businessman, in addition to his statesmanship) wrote: "Early to bed and early to rise, / Makes a man healthy, wealthy, and wise."

Modern-day Business Superheroes should take this centuries-old advice to heart. In his recent bestseller *The Greatness Guide*, Robin Sharma, one of my favorite authors and one of the planet's leading business coaches, preaches "Be wise, early rise." Sharma suggests that you should awake at either 5:00 or 6:00 a.m. and should spend the first sixty minutes of the day (the "Holy Hour," as he calls it) on "the inner you" by setting priorities, thinking big, and contemplating life. The Holy Hour, he claims, "infuses every remaining minute of your day with a perspective that elevates each area of your life."

I have found this to be especially applicable for Business Superheroes, who, like their crime-fighting brethren, must keep odd hours to succeed.

SUPERHERO EXERCISE 4

Rise Early

Try this for a week:

1. Set your alarm for sixty minutes earlier than usual.
2. When it rings, jump out of bed to greet the day.
3. Then spend the majority of the first hour of the day on something you like.

   That book you've been meaning to read
   That painting you have been wanting to finish
   A leisurely breakfast at an outdoor café

4. Reserve the last fifteen minutes of the hour for organizing the rest of your day.

The first few days will be hard, but once you get through them your new routine will yield great rewards.

GOLDEN RULE 8: BE READY FOR TEAM-UPS

No matter who you are, be it boss or receptionist. No matter where you work, be it a law firm or a fruit stand. No matter your level of experience, be you a young buck or a well-worn veteran. One thing will always be true—*you can't do it all yourself.*

Like their costumed counterparts, Business Superheroes often rely on others. And if that is true for ultra-loners like Batman (who has Commissioner Gordon to feed him intel on the bad guys, a boy wonder sidekick to help his cause, and a butler to keep his life in order), shouldn't it be true for you?

Superhero team-ups are a staple of the comic industry. So much so that both of the big two publishers (DC Comics and Marvel Comics) have historically had a series featuring nothing but team-ups. (Marvel had the aptly named *Marvel Team-Up*, while DC opted for the more subtle *The Brave and the Bold.*)

During the Silver Age of Comics (from the late 1950s to the 1970s), irrespective of the two characters involved in a given month's issue, most superhero team-ups were structured according to the following pattern:

1. Hero 1 is pursuing a mission.
2. Hero 2 is pursuing a mission.
3. Their paths cross, and a fight breaks out due to misunderstanding.
4. The fight continues, introducing the possibility of stalemate or the threat of mutual destruction.
5. Both heroes realize they are stronger together than individually and decide to resolve their conflict and team up.
6. They achieve greater success in their missions than they could have done individually.
7. All is well . . . until the next time.

As Business Superheroes, you need to avoid the initial fight at all costs. Unfortunately, more often than not, when the opportunity to team up arises, many young businesspeople immediately perceive their potential ally as a threat instead of seeing the team-up for what it truly is—an opportunity for growth.

Why Team-Ups Are Important to Business Superheroes

There are lots of reasons why you, the Business Superhero-in-Training, should actively pursue both formal team-ups (external strategic alliances) and informal team-ups (internal ad hoc work groups). The potential benefits include:

- ⋆ By working with others, you can learn from them (see Chapter 7).
- ⋆ By working with others, you can expand your network (see Golden Rule 9: Patrol often).
- ⋆ By working with others, you can take on tasks too large for an individual and achieve rewards you could not have gained alone (see Chapter 19).
- ⋆ By working with others, you can expand the range of possible solutions and overcome problems that may be intractable when working solo.

But most of all, I think the power of team-ups can be best summed up by this maxim:

If you and I each exchange one dollar,
Then, in the end, we both have one dollar.
If you and I each exchange one idea,
Then in the end, we both have two ideas.

The reason this maxim applies here is actually much more complicated than most people realize. When I first started university, I sat in an economics 101 lecture, during which the professor announced unequivocally that the Law of Scarcity rules all. The Law of Scarcity in economics is simply this: When people believe that something they desire is available in only limited quantity, the value they place on that thing becomes much greater than if that item were widely available. This law was central to the economic theory of Lionel Robbins, who, in an influential 1932 essay, defined economics as "the science which studies human behavior as a relationship between ends and scarce means which have alternative uses."

However, being an irreverent young man (then and now) I contend that the professor—and possibly even Robbins—may not be entirely correct. I believe that the Law of Scarcity is not universal. Take knowledge, love, hate, and even medical cures. When shared, the value of these items grows exponentially. The same can be true of some commodities as well, like software programs. The value of the instant messaging medium—a way to pass e-notes between people—actually grows when shared, as does the value of the products that people use to that end. In fact, in all these cases there is almost an "Inverse Rule of Scarcity," meaning that the more certain things (love, ideas, and so on) are shared, the more value they can obtain and provide.

Align and Grow: How to Make the Most of Team-Ups

So coming back to team-ups in business, Business Superheroes need to worry less about scarcity and hoarding resources and more about teaming up and expanding resources. The key, of course, is to ensure that you maximize the value of the team-up. To do so, try some of the following:

- Avoid at all costs being closed or negative toward the team-up. Learn your lesson from the team-ups of the Silver Age of Comics and try to move immediately beyond the hero vs. hero stage.
- Try to see the opportunity from the other person's perspective. I advise all my clients and mentees to always start their strategizing with the Natural Law of Business—people will almost always do what is in their enlightened self-interest—and go from there (see Chapter 4).
- Once you've determined what's in it for the other guy, you need to identify the goals that you hope to achieve

from the relationship. If you're stumped, reread the list of potential benefits of team-ups, keeping your particular alliance in mind.

* Once you know what both parties are seeking, you need to ensure that you align your activities so you will both get what you need, if not necessarily what you dream of. This is commonly referred to as a win-win situation.
* Finally, you need to spend time considering the range of all possible outcomes (see Chapter 28), to ensure you have fully examined the potential benefits and pitfalls of the opportunity.
* Once the team-up is over, keep the lines of communication open. This will ensure that you are able to call on your new partner again, should suitable opportunities present themselves. After his team-up with Superman, Batman chose to resume his status as the archetypal superhero loner, yet the Batmobile always had a special button that could be used to call Superman whenever the situation demanded it.

If you follow this advice for both formal and informal team-ups, you should ensure victory for all. And remember, the X-Men weren't built in a day. Good relationships need to be nurtured, so if you want to get the most out of team-ups, align today so that you can grow tomorrow.

GOLDEN RULE 9: PATROL OFTEN

Most superheroes go on patrol. Spider-Man swings through Manhattan looking for trouble. Batman tours Gotham in the Batmobile, ensuring its citizens' safety. Even Superman uses his superhearing to monitor the police band. They do this to increase the probability that they will be in the right place at the right time. Their goal, of course, is to thwart villainy.

Business Superheroes, whose goal should be ethical business success, likewise need to set themselves up to be in the right place at the right time when opportunity presents itself. The easiest way for Business Superheroes to do this is to network, network, and then network some more.

When it comes to networking, I recommend the following MO or plan of attack:

1. Compile a list of industry events (breakfasts, conferences, lunch-and-learns) that are relevant to you. To do this:
   - A. Do an Internet search.
   - B. Ask others at work what events they attend. (Ask your peers, bosses, staff who report to you, significant customers, and even competitors.)
2. Give each event on your list a score, rating each of the following three criteria on a scale of 1 to 5:
   - A. **Participation.** Who else participates? Be sure to consider attendees, sponsors, and speakers. Give a 5 to

events that will be filled with people whom you'd like in your network, and a 1 to events in which very few targets for your network are likely to attend.

B. **Content.** Look to previous agenda and marketing promotions. See how many topics listed appeal to you. Give a 5 to events in which almost all of the listed topics are of interest to you and a 1 to those that have none.

C. **Leverage.** Examine your ability to get involved. Business Superheroes don't just attend networking events—they get involved. So rank your ability to assume some leadership position over time. Through firsthand experience, I have learned that the value of a networking event I participate in is much greater than that of one I simply attend. Rank an event as 5 if you could assume a leadership role within eighteen months. Rank the event as 1 if there is little or no chance for you to be more than an attendee in the foreseeable future.

3. Now sit down with your partner, boss, mentor, and/or sidekick and examine your findings. Pick one or two events that have the highest overall scores. These will be your starting points.
4. Attend these events. Confirm that your initial scores helped you pick beneficial gatherings.
5. Once you have determined that these events are your best starting point, meet with the administrator of each event

(usually, this is a mid-level employee) and offer to volunteer. Networking organizations are for the most part volunteer based, so there is usually no shortage of tasks available to those willing to help.

6. Work your way up the food chain, until you are in a leadership position and fully enabled to leverage your new network.
7. Repeat with other, lower-ranking events, as your time permits.

To illustrate the success of this technique, let me tell you about Casey. Casey was a young entrepreneur, fresh out of university and looking to raise capital for his startup. After reading my first book, *Wise Words: Lessons in Entrepreneurship & Venture Capital*, Casey understood that venture capital and angel investment is a business of relationships. He knew that if he wanted to raise the $2 million he needed, he would have to network. However, he was fresh out of school and could barely afford to attend local networking events. So following the MO just outlined, Casey focused on two events—the local board of trade's Venture Capital Breakfast Series and the National Financing Forum. Casey volunteered for both, taking on all the low-level "joe jobs" available, including being an usher and doorman. Sounds unbecoming of a superhero, does it not?

But it wasn't. As a doorman, Casey got to greet everyone, make himself visible, arrive early, and stay late. He also got to attend all these events for *free*. Then, when it came time for him to apply to present at these events, he was already well known, and many of the people he had met in his doorman role spoke in his favor. To make a long story short, he got multiple offers of funding, took the best, and went on to build a great company.

GOLDEN RULE 10: OVERCOME ADVERSITY

Benjamin Franklin said that "in this world nothing is certain but death and taxes." I'd like to add *adversity* to that list. No one, including Business Superheroes, can go through life without facing adversity. The key is not how much adversity you experience, but how you handle those experiences and how you choose to be shaped by them.

Matt Murdock, more commonly known as Daredevil in superhero circles, was the son of the famous boxer "Battlin' Jack" Murdock, who was a contender in the last throes of his professional career when the story of Daredevil begins.

In his retelling of Daredevil's origins, comic artist/writer extraordinaire Frank Miller (who also penned many masterpieces including *Batman: The Dark Knight Returns*, *Sin City*, and *300*) included a quotation that I've never forgotten since I first read it in those pages. Let me set the scene for you: It takes place hours before Jack Murdock is killed by the Mafia for not taking a dive. Jack is trying to comfort his son (the future Daredevil), who was recently blinded in a toxic spill. Jack takes Matt aside and shares a piece of wisdom more commonly associated with Vince

Lombardi,* saying: "Son, the measure of a man isn't how many times he gets knocked down, the measure of a man is how many times he gets up." That quote has always stuck with me as one of the keystones of being a Business Superhero. Adversity will come, but how you handle it—that's what you will be measured by.

I discuss this topic extensively throughout the book. When I discuss Green Lantern (Chapter 3), I talk about the need to overcome the fear of failure. When I analyze Thor (Chapter 9), I consider how the founders of Home Depot turned their adversity (getting fired) into the start of their greatest success. You'll even see how Batgirl became a much more powerful superhero, called Oracle, by overcoming her confinement to a wheelchair (Chapter 22).

I too have faced adversity. No, I've never been shot by the Joker or beaten to a pulp by Doomsday, but I have had my fair share of struggles, and I am convinced that it was those struggles that led me to strive for even greater heights. So when business doesn't go your way, remember Battlin' Jack's words and pick yourself up. After all, as leadership guru Robin Sharma says, "Every challenge is nothing more than a chance to make things better."

Throughout this book, you will see that the true essence of a hero isn't the powers or the costume, but the choices made. Some, when faced with adversity, crumble. Others, including

*Football coach Vince Lombardi is himself something of a superhero to many in the business and leadership communities, as evidenced by the number of books that apply his strategies and inspirational techniques to a business context.

superheroes, rise to the occasion and turn adversity into opportunity. But at the heart of almost all heroes lies an inability to be held down, knocked back, or forced to quit.

Take at look at some of these famous failures compiled by CreatingMinds.org:

- ★ Walt Disney was fired by the editor of a newspaper, who claimed that he had "no good ideas."
- ★ When Thomas Edison was a boy, his teacher told him he was "too stupid to learn anything."
- ★ Albert Einstein was four years old before he spoke. He spoke haltingly until nine years of age. He was advised to drop out of high school because his teachers told him he would never amount to much.
- ★ Henry Ford's first two automobile businesses failed.
- ★ The early inventions of Bill Hewlett and Dave Packard included a lettuce-picking machine and an electric weight-loss machine.
- ★ Ray Krok failed as a real estate salesperson before discovering the McDonald's idea.
- ★ R. H. Macy failed seven times before his New York store finally caught on.
- ★ Akio Morita and Masaru Ibuka sold only 100 units of their original product—a faulty automatic rice cooker that burned the rice. Later, they built a cheap tape recorder for use in Japanese schools. This was the foundation of Sony.

* F. W. Woolworth got a job in a dry-goods store when he was twenty-one, but his employer would not let him wait on customers because he "didn't have enough sense."

Additionally, in her 1997 commencement address to Wellesley College, Oprah Winfrey recounted that she got fired from her job as a Baltimore news anchor because she wasn't "fit for television." She claims to have been demoted in 1978 to the position of . . . talk show host.

Each of these people was dubbed a "failure," yet all of them persevered and went on to become iconic Business Superheroes in their own right.

One final thought that I hope will resonate with you: Although failure sucks, it is nevertheless a respectable accomplishment in and of itself. If you fail, it means you tried. If you never fail, it usually means that you lack the conviction needed to push yourself to ever-greater heights. I once interviewed a world champion mixed martial arts fighter. In his youth, he was a world champion; but age is no more kind to athletes than their opponents are, and he ended his career with a series of losses. When I asked him how losing made him feel, he responded: "If you never lose a fight, you aren't fighting tough enough guys." That's the point that Business Superheroes embrace: Dark clouds aren't valuable only for their silver linings; they are themselves proof that you are living up to your highest ideals and still fighting the right battles.

PART II

LESSONS FROM THE LEGENDS

In Part I, I laid out the Ten Golden Rules that make up the introductory course to becoming a Business Superhero. In this part, I zero in on some of the most beloved comic icons of the twentieth century—including Superman, Batman, Thor, and Spider-Man—to discuss what they can teach up-and-coming Business Superheroes. We'll also delve into some lesser-known characters, such as Deadman, Oracle, and Madrox the Multiple Man, to learn what they too can teach us about the world of business. So grab your cape, your cowl, and your pen (for taking notes) and start turning the pages.

BATMAN: PREPARATION LEADS TO SUCCESS

Batman (or Bat-Man, according to the original spelling) first struck terror into the hearts of criminals in 1939—in *Detective Comics* #27, specifically—before going on to become one of DC Comics' most recognizable icons.

WHO IS BATMAN?

The second member of DC Comics' "Big Three," alongside Superman and Wonder Woman, Batman was created by Bob Kane and (the often overlooked and more often undercredited) Bill Finger. Batman was originally an amalgamation of diverse influences: Leonardo da Vinci's ornithopter, director Roland West's *The Bat Whispers*, Zorro, and the Shadow. But less important than his origins is what Batman has since gone on to become.

The Dark Knight, as his devoted fans often describe him,

Although Bruce Wayne, Batman's alter ego, was spurred to don his cape and cowl after witnessing the death of his parents when he was a young child, many devotees argue that it is the Batman visage that is the superhero's true face and it's Bruce Wayne that is the assumed identity.

epitomizes what one man can become with unlimited resources, the right motivation, and, above all, an overwhelming commitment and focus. In his seventy-year comic book career, Batman has repeatedly been cited as the most dangerous of heroes. Readers were reminded of his fearsome powers in issue #4 of Frank Miller's epic 1986 miniseries *The Dark Knight Returns*, in which the Caped Crusader put a thoroughly humiliating beat-down on none other than the Man of Steel himself—Superman.

WHY DOES BATMAN MATTER?

Batman serves as a unique counterbalance to Superman. The former is human, using only his skills and tools to fight crime; the latter is an alien imbued with almost godlike powers. The former hides his human frailty beneath a dark cloak; the latter hides his superhuman strength behind a clumsy manner and glasses. The former is cold, rational, calculating, and willing to do whatever it takes; the latter is seen as the great blue Boy Scout, more concerned with appearances and moral niceties than willing to enter the morally ambiguous ground where the pursuit of justice can occasionally lead.

Over the years, and particularly for Business Superheroes, Batman has shown fans both the sacrifices demanded by justice and the power of relentless dedication. He has been rewarded with immortality in radio shows, a dozen live-action and animated TV shows, a half dozen full-length animated features, Underoos, T-shirts, lunch boxes, and more action figures than you can shake a stick at.

LESSON 1 What Can You Learn from Batman?
Lesson: Success Is 90 Percent Preparation

Batman has no supernatural powers. Instead, he trains his body and mind to the edge of perfection and then prepares for all eventualities. He is not alone in this. Dale Carnegie (see Chapter 4) once remarked, “If you plan for the worst, only good things can happen.” The same is true in business. In fact, I’ll go one step further and suggest that the Dark Knight’s example permits us to modify Carnegie’s statement, to read: “If you plan, then only good things can happen.”

Too many people, in my estimation, undertake too little preparation. Before every big meeting, before every interview, before every presentation, I first invest extensive amounts of time in thinking through all of the possible outcomes and addressing each in due course. Can I do this in all cases? Of course not, but it's possible in 90 percent of situations. But note, there is a big difference between preparing for something and worrying about something. The former is vital; the latter, a waste.

Unfortunately, most people spend the hours and minutes before a noteworthy event worrying rather than preparing. I've never fully understood this. Energy put into preparing for eventualities that may not come to pass is time well spent. Worrying about contingencies that are beyond your control is not. Remember the Serenity Prayer, which is most commonly rendered as:

God grant me the serenity to accept the things I cannot change,
courage to change the things I can,
and the wisdom to know the difference.

LESSON 2 What Can You Learn from Batman?

Lesson: Have the Right Tools

Batarangs, smoke bombs, grappling hooks, night-vision goggles: Batman has them all, for he knows the value of having the right tools on hand. Business Superheroes often fail not for lack of trying or even for want of skill but because they are trying to drive a nail with a screwdriver. You need the right tools, not just to fight crime but to accomplish any complex task. In the business world, our most valuable tool is information, without which we can accomplish virtually none of our goals. Yet managers worldwide consistently struggle to make key decisions without the data they need.

Information is our primary tool because it alone permits us to determine which other tools (whether they be skills, materials, or additional resources) are necessary for a specific task. Business Superheroes should thus start any decision-making process by defining the problem, then they should determine what information and resources are needed. Superheroes make sure they are prepared before embarking on a course of action. If you follow any strategy other than Batman's own process of cold reason and cautious preparation, you risk being ill-equipped and may find yourself falling without a bat-net to save you!

LESSON 3 What Can You Learn from Batman?

Lesson: Even Loners Need Support

Batman draws extensively on the support of Alfred, the butler; Commissioner Gordon; and, of course, his sidekick, Robin (see Chapter 7), illustrating that even a die-hard loner vigilante understands the power of a support network.

The same should be true for any Business Superhero as well. To some, the receptionist is just a person to nod to in the morning. Others harness that person's role as a "director of first impressions" and information broker. Similarly, to some, human resource (HR) managers are the people you ask about benefits, whereas others see HR personnel as a source of valuable strategic information (such as which departments are expanding) that may shape future opportunities.

Regardless, if even a loner like Batman needs allies, then accept that you do too. Once you understand this, you should determine which people would be the most welcome additions to your team. In the years that I worked at Ernst & Young, I found two of my best allies to be the mail guy and the information technology (IT) support person. The former always seemed to be the first to know any internal developments, and the latter always seemed to ensure my computer was the best available. Coincidence? I think not.

So ask yourself, Whom do I want on my "bat team"? With whom do I want to work? Which of my peers would make a good sidekick? Who complements my skills?

THE GREEN LANTERN: THE WILL AND THE WAY

In 1960, at the dawn of the Silver Age of Comics, DC Comics editor Julius Schwartz set out to revise and update one of his childhood favorites, a superhero named the Green Lantern. In doing so, Schwartz helped usher in the Second Age of Superheroes.

WHO IS THE GREEN LANTERN?

In the DC universe, the Green Lantern is one of 7,200 space patrolmen who make up the fabled Green Lantern Corps. Each patrolman guards a particular sector of space against evil and injustice, answering only to the omniscient race of blue-skinned aliens dubbed the Guardians of the Universe. The Lanterns are armed with their quick wit, courage, and an invincible weapon of justice called a "power ring."

This ring, powered by the wearer's willpower, can manifest its owner's imagination. With it, the bearer of the ring (often called a "Ringslinger") can fly, turn invisible and/or immaterial, be telepathic, understand any language, shoot force beams, transmute matter, and even create hard-light holograms in any shape or form (such as giant green boxing gloves, shovels, and teddy bears). Truth be told, the ring can pretty much do anything, subject to three limitations:

- It has difficulty affecting anything colored yellow (due to an impurity in the central power battery that was later overcome).
- It can hold only a limited amount of energy and thus typically needs to be recharged at a "power battery" every twenty-four hours.
- It is only as strong as its possessor's willpower.

It is this last point that truly speaks to the essence of the Green Lantern. To join the Green Lantern Corps, one need only be fearless and possess an incredibly strong will. Personal backgrounds are irrelevant. In fact, the corps is an interstellar mosaic made up of an almost infinitely assorted menagerie of sentient beings, making it a bastion of diversity.

WHY DOES THE GREEN LANTERN MATTER?

For me, the Green Lantern has always shown that with wisdom (knowing what needs to be done) and willpower (the dedication one needs to do what is needed), altering reality is possible.

This isn't just a comic book fantasy—athletes around the world have testified to the power of visualization. Michael Jordan saw his shot before he took it. Wayne Gretzky saw the winning goal before the puck left his stick. Carl Lewis imagined breaking the 100-meter world record long before he crossed the finish line. These athletes claim that by visualizing the outcome they desire they are actually able to increase the probability of its occurrence, thus providing compelling evidence in support of the power of visualization.

Similarly, the power of visualization was also a cornerstone of Nike cofounder Bill Bowerman's success. In both his career as the head coach of University of Oregon's track team and at Nike, Bowerman knew the power of visualization—a technique he passed on to his athletes and managers. Did it work? Oregon's track-and-field team had twenty-three winning seasons in the twenty-four years he was head coach, and the team went on to win four National Collegiate Athletic Association (NCAA) titles. Bowerman achieved similar excellence in the corporate world: By 1980, sixteen years after it was founded, Nike had more than 50 percent of the market share in athletic shoes, proving the power of visualization in business.

In her 2006 bestseller *The Secret*, Rhonda Byrne dubbed this theory the "Law of Attraction." Well, this theory is not a revolutionary one—the idea that positive thoughts can produce positive outcomes dates back thousands of years. Buddha stated, "All that we are is the result of what we have thought." Furthermore, several contemporary thinkers believe that this may be more than a simple platitude and may actually have scientific basis in the principles that underlie quantum physics. All evidence aside, there is much commonsense merit in visualizing your desired outcome before pursuing it. After all, if you can't believe it, how can you possibly be prepared to receive it?

The other aspect of the Green Lantern that has always fascinated me is the fact that each member of the corps had to be fearless. As a child, I thought that meant that my heroes were actually immune to anxiety or trepidation. But today, the stories of these Emerald Warriors have shown me that fearlessness is in fact a more nuanced emotion than I had originally believed—one best described by paraphrasing Ambrose Redmoon: To be fearless is not to be without fear; it is to understand fear, to know fear, and to continue on in spite of and in the face of what you fear.

LESSON 1 What Can You Learn from the Green Lantern?

Lesson: Match Wits with Your Fear

Everyone fears something. Some fears, like claustrophobia (the fear of being unable to escape a confining situation), are seemingly irrational and may be the result of childhood trauma or neurosis. These sorts of fears are better left to the therapist. I want to deal with the other type of fear—the fear that prevents you from pursuing tasks you know you should, like speaking up at a meeting, asking for a raise, or agreeing to lead your team.

Let me be clear on this. In my mind at least, there is nothing wrong with being afraid, but there is everything wrong with letting that fear prevent you from pursuing what you know is right. Fear has its place (it prevents us from courting danger recklessly), but you have to decide how much control over your actions you want that fear to have. Nvidia's founder Jen-Hsun Huang knew fear would be at the heart of his now globally dominant computer chip–making company. Huang claims that his fear of letting others down fueled his focus and was crucial to his successful creation of the $5 billion company. Indeed, Huang knows something about fear: Upon immigration to the United States when he was ten years old, Huang's family decided to enroll the boy in a prep school; they unintentionally enrolled him in a reform school for juvenile delinquents, instead. It was there that Huang learned to "overcome great fear."

Oprah Winfrey, my sister's favorite Business Superhero, also learned early on that overcoming fear was a key component to success. Oprah, who is consistently voted one of the most powerful women in America, learned to reject fear. She espouses that the "true test of courage is to be afraid and to go ahead and do it anyway."

SUPERHERO EXERCISE 5

Preparing to Battle against Fear

Use the example of the Green Lantern (or Oprah) to know and overcome your fear by undertaking the following exercise. Make four lists, one for each of the following:

Ambition. What is it that you want to do to fulfill your goals?
Internal obstacle. What fear prevents you from meeting your goals?
Origins. Where does your fear originate?
Strategies. How else, other than facing it head-on, can you overcome your fear? What resources would you need?

Take the time to look at the relationships among the items on your lists to see which fears hinder a number of your goals or which might have common solutions. Remember that the object is not to eliminate the fear but to eliminate its power over your ability to act in the pursuit of your goals and ideals.

And when in doubt, ask yourself, What would the Green Lantern do?

LESSON 2 What Can You Learn from the Green Lantern?

Lesson: Wisdom + Willpower = Results

Everyone wants a better life, world, and/or job. Few know how to get what they desire. The Green Lantern teaches us that to shape your reality, you need two things:

* **Wisdom.** Knowing what you need to do
* **Willpower.** Having the courage to do what is needed

Let's say you want to lose weight.

* You need the wisdom to understand that you lose weight when the calories you burn exceed the calories you take in. Thus realize that you must either lower your calorie intake (by cutting out sweets, for example) or increase the calories you burn (such as by exercising more).
* You need the willpower to follow through, each and every day, exercising regularly and monitoring your calories. Have the courage to stick to your plan, even though it is hard.

As you can see, being wise enough to know what to do is not enough—you need to have the willpower to pursue your plan and the dedication to keep at it. This is true whether you want to be promoted, to obtain a capital infusion for your business's growth, or to lose your beer belly.

LESSON 3 What Can You Learn from the Green Lantern?

Lesson: Remember to Recharge Your Battery

The Green Lantern shows us that even the most powerful tool in the universe has its limits. The same is true with your most powerful personal tool, your brain. No matter who you are, or what you do, everyone needs downtime.

For some this can be a simple nap, whereas for others it can be a weekend at the cottage. Regardless of what it is for you, you need to schedule regular breaks from your duties, or you risk running out of power when you need it most.

Seems like a simple lesson, yes? Yet many high-performing executives routinely suffer from burnout, the epitome of running out of energy. How is it that these people, who have demonstrated remarkable proficiency at managing corporate resources, should have such difficulty monitoring and managing their own personal resources?

Among the high-performing CEOs I've had the pleasure to work with, this issue is a real one. However, there really is no excuse for it. After all, what is the point of winning the battle while losing the war? Yet time and time again, I see many exhausted business superstars. When I discuss with them the need for balance, almost every single one responds with the same reasoning: "I'm too busy to rest" or "I've got way too much to take care of." My simple, yet effective, response to this has always been: "Isn't that like saying 'I'm too busy driving to get gas'?"

LESSON 4 What Can You Learn from the Green Lantern?

Lesson: Everyone Has a Boss

Bob Dylan said it best: "You're gonna have to serve somebody." All Green Lanterns report to the blue-hued immortal Guardians

THE GREEN LANTERN OF THE REAL WORLD

To me, Richard Branson is the Green Lantern of our world. Here is a man who, through the sheer force of his will, created an empire. He dropped out of school at an early age and began shaping his world through business: first through the magazine *Student*, then through Virgin Records, followed by Virgin Atlantic. His creations now include more than 200 companies operating under the Virgin brand.

On the subject of fearlessness, he is equally qualified, having traversed both the Atlantic and Pacific oceans in a hot-air balloon. These trips almost cost him his life on several occasions, yet he did not stop until he finished what he started.

On the issue of Branson's willpower, we can turn to William Whitehorn. The current president of Virgin Galactic (Branson's venture into commercial space travel) said it best about Branson: "When the chips are really down, his determination grows exponentially."

of the Universe, so even while the individual patrolmen have virtual autonomy, in the end they each have a boss to report to.

The same is true in business. CEOs report to the board of directors, entrepreneurs report to their clients, and so on. Therefore, you need to understand your bosses' own goals or motivations before you undertake their mission. So every hero (business or super) needs to know four things:

- ★ Who is your true boss?
- ★ What is his or her end goal?

* How does he or she achieve that goal?
* What does your boss need you to do to further his or her goal?

Try keeping these points in mind, or risk exposing yourself to the wrath of your "true boss."

DEADMAN: GAIN PERSPECTIVE

First there was Superman, then Batman, then Aquaman, and by the late 1960s Spider-Man, Iceman, and Ant-Man had all joined the scene. But by far my favorite of all the men was DC Comics' Deadman.

WHO IS DEADMAN?

First appearing in 1967, Deadman's origins offered readers an interesting and unique starting point. The cover of *Strange Adventures* #205 informs us that the story begins "One minute after our hero's death." Deadman tells the tale of circus acrobat Boston Brand, who was murdered during a trapeze act by the mysterious assailant known only as Hook. Resurrected by an Eastern deity named Rama Kushna, Deadman was literally a ghost: Intangible, invisible to the naked eye, and armed only with the ability to instantly inhabit (and thus control) any sentient being.

Jumping from body to body in his quest to solve his own murder, some fans believe Deadman's predicament was instrumental to the creation of the 1990s sci-fi TV show *Quantum Leap*, which similarly features an out-of-place stranger jumping from body to body to right injustice. Although Deadman never quite came out of the shadows to garner his own series, he was a long standby backup player to the Batman mythos and brought Eastern views about karma to the DC universe.

WHY DOES DEADMAN MATTER?

Besides providing a powerful venue for the innovative artistry of Neil Adams, Deadman shows the lasting relevance of the early-twentieth-century orator and founder of the self-help movement, Dale Carnegie.

Dale Carnegie, in his must-read (and still relevant) 1936 bestseller *How to Win Friends and Influence People*, teaches readers of the need to place oneself in another's shoes in an effort to better understand his or her unique perspective. Deadman does that literally! The Native American dictum "Do not judge your neighbor until you walk two moons in his moccasins" becomes demonstrated in an unusual manner by Deadman, who must inhabit another's body in order to take action. Because of his approach, this superhero provides one of the principal lessons that young Business Superheroes need to learn: the Deadman Perspective.

LESSON 1 What Can You Learn from Deadman?

Lesson: Walk in the Shoes of Another

In a world driven by a what's-in-it-for-me attitude, Deadman's need to walk a mile in another's shoes reminds up-and-coming Business Superheroes of the advantage that can be gleaned by taking time to see other peoples' perspectives.

In fact, I'd recommend applying the Deadman Principle as often as possible:

- ★ Giving a speech? Put yourself in your audience's shoes and ask, "If I were them, what would I want to take away from this?"
- ★ Entering a negotiation? Start by asking yourself what the other party's goals and BATNA* might be.
- ★ Delivering bad news? Take a moment to ask yourself how you'd like to be on the receiving end of it.

In fact, by striving to understand another's perspective before taking action, you can actually increase the probability of obtaining your desired outcome. After all, if you can articulate a clear understanding of your audience's desires and priorities, you are much more likely to predict and meet its interests and, in doing so, to align its interests and expectations with your own.

*The acronym stands for "best alternative to negotiated agreement"—a concept analyzed in Roger Fisher and William Ury's groundbreaking negotiation treatise *Getting to Yes: Negotiating Agreement Without Giving In.*

DEADMAN OF THE REAL WORLD

After reading this chapter, you can no doubt guess whom I'd name "Deadman of the Real World": Dale Carnegie. Carnegie (1888–1955) was born in Missouri, and his motivational classic *How to Win Friends and Influence People* has sold more than 15 million copies and has been translated into fifteen languages since its publication in 1936.

Before David Allen, Anthony Robbins, and Wayne Dyer, there was Carnegie. In fact, *A&E Biography* recently named him "the father of the self-help movement."

Besides articulating the principles of effective communication and negotiation that are illustrated throughout this chapter, many suggest that his faith in the ability to improve one's life and relationships through communication had a deeper philosophical foundation in the Responsibility Assumption, a credo of personal empowerment that maintains that we control to some degree the different events that shape our lives. This assertion of the power of positive thinking is in turn closely related to the Law of Attraction (discussed in Chapter 3).

SPAWN: THINK BEFORE YOU ACT

In 1992, Spawn became a defining title of the Dark Age of Comics. In this age, which began in the mid-1980s, comics took a dark turn, most notably brought on by the works of Alan Moore (*The Watchmen, V for Vendetta, Miracleman*) and Frank Miller (*Sin City, Dark Knight Returns*). Superheroes became darker, more violent, and far less wholesome than in previous eras. During this age, a handful of top artists and writers broke away from DC Comics and Marvel Comics to form Image Comics. (For more on the Four Ages of Comics, see "Comic Book History 101.")

Spawn was Image's best-known and most consistently popular character (having also given rise to HBO's adult cartoon of the same name and the reasonably well-made 1997 movie from New Line Cinema). The Dark Age continued until early 2002, when the comic book world saw a resurgence of less realistic, more traditionally heroic characters, in what is being dubbed the Modern Age of Comics.

WHO IS SPAWN?

Spawn's story is that of an antihero. Even before donning a cape and cowl, the character was darkly skewed.

Spawn's beginnings are found in the legend of Al Simmons, a ruthless, corrupt CIA mercenary who is killed by his boss to cover up even deeper corruption. Post-death, Simmons makes a deal with the devil himself, trading his soul for a return ticket to earth, to see his wife and true love, Wanda.

As has been the case for centuries in literature, deals with the devil rarely work out, and Simmons finds himself returned to earth five years later as a horribly disfigured hell-spawn filled with magical superpowers, but with little memory of his previous life. Spawn also finds that his wife has moved on, marrying Simmons's best friend, who in turn was involved in his murder. (As I said, this was a dark time for superhero comics.)

WHY DOES SPAWN MATTER?

Besides ushering in the Dark Age of Comics and helping found the first new sustainable comic book company in years, Spawn became the most valuable comic character not owned by either DC Comics or Marvel Comics.

For Business Superheroes, Spawn serves as a reminder that

we should be careful what we wish for and even more careful in the deals we make with the devil. Spawn also shows the power of karma in business.

LESSON 1 What Can You Learn from Spawn?

Lesson: Karma's a Bitch

The definition of *karma* differs according to religious or philosophical tradition, but karma generally denotes a belief that one's life experiences are clearly influenced by one's actions. Thus doing wrong to others will lead to some harm happening to you in the future.

Early on in my career, I was mentored by John Goudey, one of Ernst & Young's biggest rainmakers. John would often remind me that "the business world was in fact a very small place" and that "actions chosen poorly can often come back to haunt you." This fact was proven time and time again, as my career expanded.

No matter the industry that you work in, remember that you have to live with your actions and their consequences and that someday you will likely have to defend them. As such, always pursue good business karma. The easiest way to do this is to ensure that all your actions can survive the "light of day" test—namely, don't do anything you wouldn't be proud of should news of it reach the light of day.

So wherever possible, offer a hand to colleagues, clients, and even competitors. In doing so, you will not only increase your position as a Business Superhero, you will bank karma for later. After all, more often than not, you will run into those people again and—who knows—at that time, it may be you benefiting from their assistance.

LESSON 2 What Can You Learn from Spawn?

Lesson: Be Careful What You Wish For

Spawn is also a powerful reminder that you should be careful what you wish for because it may come true. This oft-cited message suggests that one should fully contemplate a pact before entering into it. This idea that you should be careful what you wish for may predate even the Greek myth of King Midas, although a more recent updating of the legend can be found in William Wymark Jacobs's story "The Monkey's Paw," which appeared in *Harper's Monthly* in 1902.

Jacobs's story—which was revisited in the 1991 *Simpsons* Halloween special, "Treehouse of Horror II"—tells of a talisman shaped like a monkey's paw, which grants the holder three wishes, although each wish comes at an onerous price. *Spawn* #1 (which coincidentally came out about six months after the *Simpsons* special aired) reenacts this myth, granting Al Simmons's wish to see his wife again, but at a horrible cost: His humanity.

Now while I doubt many Business Superheroes will literally

be offered magical power for their souls, but figuratively . . . well, that's another story. In business, we are often asked to pursue courses of action that compromise our souls. Even indirectly, we are almost daily faced with easier roads to success, if only we were willing to compromise our ethics. Well, as Spawn shows us, we should be careful what we wish for because we just might get it.

SUPERMAN: KNOW YOUR WEAKNESS

It's a bird. It's a plane. It's the last son of Krypton! Part of the American Zeitgeist since Superman's debut in 1938 in *Action Comics* #1, the mythos of the Man of Steel continues today, making him one of superherodom's greatest symbols.

WHO IS SUPERMAN?

You likely remember the story about the baby whose parents send him far away because his life is in danger. They send him to a place where he will live as prince among men and where he will have powers far beyond the scope of ordinary people. This story first arrived in our culture thousands of years ago—in the tale of Moses in Egypt. It is also the foundation for the Superman mythos.

Superman is the story of Kal-El, the last son of Krypton, rocketed to Earth by his parents only moments before their home

planet explodes. Raised by farmers in Kansas, Superman comes to stand for "Truth, Justice, and the American Way." He adopts the secret identity of Clark Kent, ace reporter for the *Daily Planet*. While working for the paper, he meets, falls in love with, and eventually marries Lois Lane.

During the Dark Age of Comics, Superman was pretty much used, abused, and then abused some more. In fact, during the period of 1993–2004, the Man of Steel:

- ⋆ Dies
- ⋆ Is resurrected as four different possible characters, including Superboy and Steel
- ⋆ Returns with hippie hair (I kid you not)
- ⋆ Becomes an energy creature
- ⋆ Becomes two energy creatures
- ⋆ Gets married

At DC Comics, secret identities are often two first names: Superman is Clark Kent. Batman is Bruce Wayne. The Flash is Barry Allan. The Green Lantern is Hal Jordan. At Marvel, on the other hand, alliteration is all the rage when it comes to secret identities: Spider-Man is Peter Parker. Daredevil is Matt Murdock. Hulk is Bruce Banner.

More recently, in the Modern Age, Supes gets a haircut and is placed exactly back where he started, as the current Modern Age big guns in the DC universe turn their sights on Silver Age favorites like the Green Arrow and the Green Lantern.

WHY DOES SUPERMAN MATTER?

Superman's standard is held in great respect by both fans and other superheroes alike. Proof of point? Nightwing. After serving as Batman's partner for more than ten years (in continuity), Dick Grayson eventually opts to emerge from the shadow of his mentor, Batman, and become his own man.

To do that, Dick Grayson gives up his Robin identity and searches for a new costume and brand. After much thought, Grayson chooses a costume inspired by a Kryptonian myth, Nightwing (see Chapter 7 for more).

Need more proof of Superman's role as benchmark for other heroes? In the chronology of the DC universe, 1,000 years after his death (and rebirth) the legend of Superman inspires a handful of kids from across the universe to fight for justice as the Legion of Super-Heroes (see Chapter 27).

LESSON 1 What Can You Learn from Superman?

Lesson: Know Your Kryptonite

Superman stands for more than high standards. For the Business Superhero, he serves an even greater purpose: To remind us that we each have our own type of kryptonite—some thing we need to guard against vigilantly. Before Superman, this was known as a person's Achilles' heel and was a very common feature of the heroes in the Golden Age of Comics, when a number of superheroes were given a single weakness, like kryptonite. These weaknesses acted both as a plot device and as a means of keeping the characters from reaching omnipotence. In the Golden Age, the Green Lantern's ring couldn't affect wood. The ring of his Silver Age counterpart could be disrupted by either yellow or fear. Even Wonder Woman was originally written with an Achilles' heel: She lost her powers if her wrist bracelets were linked together.

However, it is not enough to be aware of your weaknesses—you have to strive to overcome them. For when you know your weakness—be it wood, yellow, or kryptonite; alcohol, flattery, or overwork—the onus is on you to protect yourself. Superman keeps a lead battle suit handy when dealing with kryptonite because lead is the only known substance to block the element.

Superman's battle suit is basically a reverse lead box that shields the superhero instead of containing the element. To some this might seem overkill, but not to me. If you know your weak point you would be foolish not to deal with it as completely as possible. After all, if you deliberately leave yourself exposed, you do not deserve to be a superhero, let alone a Business Superhero. People who are unable or unwilling to do what is clearly necessary to protect their own interests are in no position to commit themselves to protecting the safety and security (be it physical or material) of others.

For example, I have a learning disability that makes proofreading very difficult for me. It is very much my kryptonite, my fatal flaw. Left unchecked, it would kill my career as a writer. In fact, the fear of errors might keep me from writing at all. But following the lesson of Green Lantern, I overcame the fear and did what everyone else does—hired a proofreader.

I hired Dr. Jonathan Singer. I've known Jono since we were both in our teens. He is an English professor who owns the complete run of Neil Gaiman's *Sandman* comic book series, so he seemed like an ideal person to help proofread a book about Business Superheroes. I dare say that, in this case, he is the lead box that shields my writing from the kryptonite of my proofreading errors. Yes, it might seem like overkill to hire a writing professor as a proofreader, but if you want to be a Business Superhero, sometimes overkill is the only way to ensure you don't get kryptonite poisoning.

ROBIN: LEARN FROM OTHERS

Robin first joined Batman in *Detective Comics* #37 (1940). His debut was originally an effort to make Batman a lighter, more sympathetic character. DC Comics also hoped that adding a teenage sidekick would appeal to younger readers and give them a link to the oft-aloof Dark Knight.

WHO IS ROBIN?

Like his mentor, Batman, Robin is an amalgamation of many different influences, taking his name and original costume design from Robin Hood and combining it with Batman's winged motif.

Also like Batman, Robin's origin saw Dick Grayson witnessing his parents' death and then deciding to dedicate his life to fighting injustice. Unlike Batman, however, Robin was blessed with a mentor to help him channel his anger. Precisely because of

Batman's beneficial influence, Robin is often seen as a lighter, more well adjusted, more trusting version of the Dark Knight himself.

As Robin, Grayson banded together with other teenage sidekicks to form the Teen Titans (a sort of junior Justice League). It was during his tenure as their leader that Grayson truly shone, coming out of the proverbial shadow of the Bat to find his own identity. In fact, it was in 1984's *Tales of the Teen Titans* #44 that Dick Grayson officially shed his Robin identity, emerging more mature and with a different costume. Borrowing from the culture of another of his childhood mentors, Superman, Grayson named himself Nightwing, after a Batman-like vigilante from the planet Krypton. Fear not, though—the Robin moniker lives on: Since Grayson hung up his Robin cape, no fewer than four other youngsters have taken up the role.

WHY DOES ROBIN MATTER?

The Lone Ranger's sidekick, Tonto, may have debuted in 1933—predating Robin by seven years—but it was Robin who went on to inspire sidekicks the world over, including Captain America's Bucky, the Green Arrow's Speedy, and Aquaman's Aqualad.

For Business Superheroes, however, Robin demonstrates the importance of finding and learning from a mentor.

LESSON 1 What Can You Learn from Robin?
Lesson: Find a Mentor

I define a *mentor* as "someone whose hindsight becomes your foresight." Early on in my business career, my father told me that I had a choice: Learn from others or learn from the school of hard knocks. He explained that one could get ahead by looking at others' skills and learning from their experiences. Apparently, my father shares this belief with media mogul Oprah Winfrey, who claimed in her interview with the Academy of Achievement, "Everybody needs somebody to show them a way out, or a way

SUPERHERO EXERCISE 6

Find a Mentor

To find a mentor, simply seek out someone within your industry

★Who is at least ten to twenty years your senior
★Who shares similar beliefs as you
★Whom you respect
★To whom you are willing to listen

Once you have your mentor targeted, take her or him for lunch and ask directly for assistance. Lay out what it is you are seeking, how much time you will need, and the ways in which you hope to benefit from that person's influence. Many mature Business Superheroes see this as the greatest of compliments because it is tangible proof that their own commitment to excellence has inspired others to follow in their path.

up. Everybody does." So finding a mentor should be paramount for *all* future Business Superheroes. Your mentor will help you advance your skills and may prevent you from making the same mistakes as those who came before you.

CAPTAIN MARVEL: SWIPE OFTEN

After encountering a magician named Shazam, an orphaned teenage reporter is given the ability to transform a bolt of lightning into "the World's Mightiest Mortal"—an adult superhero with godlike powers. Captain Marvel, often erroneously called Shazam, has been a thorn in the side of evildoers and copyright lawyers since 1940.

WHO IS CAPTAIN MARVEL?

First published by Fawcett Comics in 1940, Captain Marvel was actually the bestselling hero of that decade, outselling Superman comics at his peak of popularity. According to *Comic Books and Graphic Novels: What to Buy*, by Michael Lavin, *Captain Marvel Adventures* sold over 14 million copies in 1944.

The origin of Captain Marvel is the story of teenage reporter Billy Batson, who is granted magical powers by a wizard named

Shazam. In one of comics' original and most enduring fantasies of adolescent empowerment, uttering the wizard's name transformed Batson into a fully grown superhero named Captain Marvel, who is imbued with superpowers attributed to mythological deities:

S	The wisdom of Solomon
H	The strength of Hercules
A	The stamina of Atlas
Z	The power of Zeus
A	The courage of Achilles
M	The speed of Mercury

Using these powers, Captain Marvel is charged with staving off the encroachment into society of humanity's greatest threat, the Seven Deadly Enemies of Man (pride, envy, greed, hatred, selfishness, laziness, and injustice).*

Now, if you can overlook the confused mythology for a moment (Solomon is a biblical character, not an ancient God; Atlas is a Greek titan; Zeus and Mercury come from different pantheons—the latter Roman, the former Greek; and, finally, Achilles was known for his virtual invulnerability, not his courage), you pretty much have the ideal superhero. Captain Marvel isn't an alien like Superman—heck, he isn't even an adult,

*The list differs from the seven deadly sins primarily by the replacement of *lust* with *injustice*, presumably to spare parents the need for any uncomfortable explanations of that sin.

he's just a kid who, when overwhelmed, can summon superpowers. Now *that's* cool.

WHY DOES CAPTAIN MARVEL MATTER?

Probably the most litigated character in comics, Captain Marvel was sued into obscurity by DC Comics in the mid-1940s. DC Comics later bought the character outright but was required to change the comic's name to *Shazam!* since Marvel Comics had acquired the trademark for the title *Captain Marvel.* In the 1950s, the issue of trademark infringement arose again when a small British publisher created Marvelman. Marvelman, who transformed from cub reporter Micky Moran to a magical powerhouse by shouting the word *Kimota* (roughly *atomic* backwards), was in turn mired in litigation. Marvel Comics sued, forcing Marvelman to become Miracleman in 1984. But that's not the end of the litigation story.

Miracleman was first written in 1982 by the now-iconic Alan Moore, who went on to usher in the Dark Age of Comics with the 1986 seminal *The Watchmen* series. In the early 1990s the now-legendary Neil Gaiman (who honed his craft in the epic *Sandman* series) took over as author. Miracleman became one of the first indications of the coming Dark Age of Comics, as Moore and Gaiman injected reality, darkness, and psychological instability into the formerly squeaky-clean hero.

This might have been the end of our poor hero's legal woes,

but thanks to Todd McFarland, it wasn't. McFarland—an icon of the Dark Age of Comics, cofounder of Image Comics, and creator of Spawn (see Chapter 5)—supposedly acquired the rights to Miracleman in 1996. Gaiman, however, also claimed rights to the works. To further complicate the matter, Gaiman and McFarland were simultaneously in dispute over two other characters (Angela and Medieval Spawn) that Gaiman had created for McFarland's Spawn series. As of this writing, the rights over Miracleman continue to be fought out in court.

LESSON 1 What Can You Learn from Captain Marvel?

Lesson: SWIPE from the Best

When I showcased Robin (in Chapter 7), I discussed the importance of mentorship for the aspiring Business Superhero. But mentorship is a long, highly invested process in which you try to learn from the experiences of others. A similar, but quicker and more self-directed method of learning from others is known as modeling, or SWIPE.

Modeling is an indirect form of mentoring, in which you attempt to emulate certain distinct characteristics of people who have proven that those characteristics work (for example, trying to model one's public speaking style after John F. Kennedy's). If you can't find a mentor or don't have the time to invest in such, modeling is a Business Superhero's next-best training tool; so closely watch those who have succeeded before you and model your approach after them.

Self-help guru Dale Carnegie is said to have used modeling to hone his public speaking abilities, basing his oratorical approach on the works of Abraham Lincoln and Ben Franklin. I've recently heard this technique referred to as SWIPE, which stands for "Steal with integrity and pride everywhere"; this term is most often associated with the process by which one industry deliberately adopts best practices from another, although it can apply equally at the personal level as an important stage in the development of a Business Superhero.

Let me be clear—SWIPE is not just for public speaking. You can SWIPE almost any idea, skill, or approach that you can make work for you:

- ★ Want to be a better team leader? Target Michael Jordan for a SWIPE, by reading a biography of him.
- ★ Want to instill a sense of pride in winning? SWIPE from Vince Lombardi's old locker-room speeches.
- ★ Want to be a better conversationalist and put people at ease? Watch those who have made a living doing just that, like Oprah Winfrey and Regis Philbin.
- ★ Want to lead social change? Study the techniques deployed by Gandhi, and SWIPE those that you can easily adopt.
- ★ Want to run a better meeting? Sit in on some public

annual shareholder meetings at a local *Fortune* 500 company. Watch how the chair balances the need to engage the crowd while managing the agenda of the meeting. If you get the chance to compare, decide which chair does the best job and figure out why.

Really, the list of things you can SWIPE is limited only by your willingness to do so and your ability to recognize and deploy the traits you want to adopt. So, if you are on your way to becoming a Business Superhero, think first about what skills you need to accomplish your predefined mission (see Chapter 13). To help you focus, pick one specific task or project you want to succeed at and visualize every possible outcome of that project. (I discuss this technique in greater detail in Chapter 28.) For every positive outcome you can visualize, write down one quality that would lead to that success. For every negative outcome, write down one quality whose absence would lead to that failure.

After you've got your list, perform an honest assessment of which of those skills listed you currently lack. Identifying your limitations is vital to making an honest assessment of your capacities (and, in turn, vital to your ability to maximize your potential). Just as you would evaluate your monetary assets before making a major investment, you need to make an honest assessment of your inner resources before taking action so you have an idea of your personal capital and deficits.

Start by selecting a single quality that you believe you lack. Pick a model from whom to SWIPE. As I mentioned, you can

SUPERHERO EXERCISE 7

Setting Up Your SWIPE

Shazam! is the magic word that turns Billy Batson into Captain Marvel, but it also serves as a touchstone—a reminder of what his superpowers are and from where (and from whom) they come. You too can have your very own magic word, with the emphasis there being on *own*, not magic. I've tried a multitude of magic words in my day, but none has (to date) granted me any sort of wonderful powers. The key, then, is come up with an acronym that

- ★Is personal to you
- ★Is easy to remember
- ★Works for you

To do this, you can either choose a generic word (*power*, *super*, *thunder*, or *cape* would work) that meets the listed criteria and then work backward, assigning a specific quality or model to each letter. Or you can go the other way, crafting a magic word after you list the skills you want to incorporate into your daily affirmation.

Here's all you need to do:

1. Jot down the attributes you wish to be known for, such as integrity, creativity, ingenuity, and leadership.
2. Make a list of famous people whom you admire for each of those attributes, for example, Katherine Graham, George Lucas, Thomas Edison, and Jack Welch.

(continued)

SUPERHERO EXERCISE 7

(continued)

3. Build your very own magic word, in this case, you could use the first letter of each last name to form GLEW.

   G The integrity of Katherine Graham
   L The creativity of George Lucas
   E The ingenuity of Thomas Edison
   W The leadership of Jack Welch

4. Print out your magic word and stick it somewhere you will see every day.

Regardless of how you come up with your magic word, it is important that you deploy it daily, keeping it at the top of your mind. Your word is a reminder of your sources of inspiration and motivation and is also an affirmation of what you can achieve by maximizing your own potential. After all, what we conceive in our heads we can achieve in reality (see Chapter 3).

start to SWIPE from a multitude of sources, so long as they're accessible. One way to test whether you've found a suitable source for a SWIPE is to revisualize your negative project outcome—only this time, add in the needed quality of the individual from whom you want to SWIPE. If your visualization leads to a different, successful outcome, then you have your SWIPE model. If not, then look to different individuals who possess that same needed quality in unique ways, until you find a model whose quality—coupled with your existing skills—leads you to visualize a successful scenario.

SWIPE from your models by analyzing how they use the skill in question. Do they use it constantly or only when necessary? When do they deploy it? What do they do as a backup when they need one? After you start putting your SWIPE into practice, you can evaluate its success by noting the situations in which you use it as well as its effects on your success.

Repeat, using the next missing quality on your list.

THOR: LOOK FOR OPPORTUNITIES

"Have at thee" and "By Odin's beard" are phrases unique to a single superhero in the comics pantheon: Marvel's Mighty Thor. A Norse god who exchanges bodies with a frail doctor in a flash of lightning, Thor is more than a little similar to DC's Captain Marvel: Both heroes' superpowers are rooted in ancient mythology, and both comics feature a superhero exchanging bodies with his weaker human form in a bolt of lightning.

WHO IS THOR?

In August 1962, Stan Lee continued his impressive run as the father of the Silver Age of Comics by inventing yet another longstanding stalwart of the Marvel universe, the god of thunder, the son of Asgard, the Mighty Thor.

Marvel's *Journey into Mystery* #83 tells the story of frail, lame Dr. Donald Blake, who (while traveling in Norway) tries to avoid an alien invasion by hiding in a cave. There, he finds an ancient walking stick inscribed with the words "Whosoever holds this hammer, if he be worthy, shall possess the power of Thor"; the stick imbues its wielder with all the power of the legendary Teutonic thunder god.

Since Thor's creation more than forty years ago, his origin and mythos have evolved and expanded. In later versions, Thor is the real entity, and Donald Blake is merely a shell in which Thor is placed by his father, Odin, as a lesson in humility. Regardless, Thor remains a fan favorite.

WHY DOES THOR MATTER?

Within Jack Kirby's somewhat psychedelic story of aliens from Saturn being thwarted by a reincarnated thunder god lies a deeper meaning for would-be Business Superheroes: See opportunity where others don't. While eluding the alien invasion, Don Blake stumbled onto a secret cave, found what looked like an ordinary walking stick, and used it to become more than he was.

LESSON 1 What Can You Learn from Thor?

Lesson: See Opportunity Where Others Don't

Business Superheroes need always to scan their environment for opportunity. And while opportunity comes in all shapes, I encourage Business Superheroes to focus on the *when*, not the what.

In the introductory tale, Blake could have found Thor's disguised magical hammer only during a moment of crisis, when he was obliged to resort to extraordinary measures in response to an extraordinary situation. This to me illustrates what Chin-Ning Chu, one of the world's leading experts on business strategy, has long stated:

> *Without the strength to endure the crisis, one will not see the opportunity within.*
> *It is within the process of endurance that opportunity reveals itself.*

At the risk of perpetuating an error, I'll repeat the widespread belief that the Chinese word for "crisis" is made up of two characters: *danger + opportunity*. While some Eastern language scholars dispute this claim, the idea contains a symbolic truth, if not a literal one: Within every crisis lies both danger and opportunity. Your job, as a Business Superhero, is to mitigate the former and maximize the latter.

When I introduced Golden Rule 10: Overcome adversity—I noted that surmounting obstacles is a requirement for all superheroes, including those in business. Chu's philosophy goes one step further: Her take on crisis is that it may very well be the best time to spot opportunity. This has proven itself in my life many times over.

Several years ago, I was chairing a national venture fair. The fair was extremely profitable, but its parent organization was not and eventually folded. This in turn caused a crisis in the entrepreneurial community because the event had become quite important: Companies attending the fair had raised more than $1 billion in venture capital for innovation.

However, as Chu purports, crisis can lead to opportunity. So, seeing an opportunity emerge with the dissolution of the venture fair's parent company, I teamed up with the president of a leading event management company and the president of the national venture capital association and relaunched the fair under a new brand. From there, as Thor would say, it was "Onward to victory!" In the end, the event was bigger, better, and more profitable than it had been before, and my own role as a leader in the venture capital community had become consolidated.

Another of my favorite real-life parables on opportunity from crisis is the story of Home Depot, which was founded by Arthur Blank and Bernie Marcus only *after* they lost their jobs running Handy Dan Home Centers in 1978. Three decades later, their little project has had over $90 billion in sales.

While their firing from Handy Dan is rumored to have been devastating, the two regularly cite that crisis as, paradoxically, the very event that precipitated their success.

HELLBOY: CREATE YOUR DESTINY

At the 1993 San Diego Comic-Com convention, artist/writer extraordinaire Mike Mignola introduced a demonic character who would change the world of comics forever.

WHO IS HELLBOY?

Summoned to Earth during the tail end of World War II by Nazi occultists who seek the ultimate weapon, Hellboy is adopted and raised by an Allied scientist who participated in the military raid that defeated the Nazi plot.

Hellboy, with his trademark filed-off horn stumps, red skin, and stone right hand, was then part of the founding of the Bureau for Paranormal Research and Defense, a nongovernmental agency that investigates "things that go bump in the night."

It is less Hellboy's red skin than his blue-collar attitude and personality that seem to make him stand out fr‹ n other modern superheroes. Hellboy likes cigars, kittens, and pancakes more than he enjoys engaging in huge battles with monsters or fighting evil. In his mind, working as "the world's leading paranormal investigator" is as commonplace as being a bus driver. Mignola often juxtaposes Hellboy's trademark nonchalant, unflappable manner against the most horrific and unsettling battles.

But Hellboy is more than just a cool character. Hellboy is also one of the most significant and successful independent titles brought to market by Dark Horse Comics. In the last ten years, Hellboy has been featured in two full-length animated DVDs, an unpublished video game, two blockbuster feature-length films, and more than five collected volumes of stories. Through this broad multimedia success, Hellboy helped show the potential benefits of letting creators own their own property: One of the ways that Dark Horse had originally distinguished itself from DC and Marvel was by allowing its creators comparatively free rein and direct ownership of the properties they created.

WHY DOES HELLBOY MATTER?

Besides inspiring a revival of comics' pulp roots and showing creators the benefits of retaining ownership of their characters, Hellboy serves to remind Business Superheroes that they, and they alone, control their destiny.

From the very beginning, a recurring theme in Hellboy is the appropriately theological question of free will vs. fate. Hellboy was originally a half demon who was brought to Earth by the Nazis in an attempt to usher in Ragnarok (the destruction of the world). Despite this plan's failure, Hellboy continues to be put in situations in which his demonic nature is at odds with his more human upbringing. Yet Hellboy is unwavering in his belief that his destiny is his and his alone to set.

LESSON 1 What Can You Learn from Hellboy?

Lesson: You Make Your Own Destiny

Like Hellboy, Business Superheroes are often faced with pressure to become what others want them to be. In fact, it is often much easier to go with the flow than to stand up and create your own path. That's why there are more employees than entrepreneurs in the world.

Hellboy reminds us that our path in life is just that—ours, and while it will be shaped and affected by outside forces, it is the decisions we make that make us the superheroes we want to be. My favorite example of this comes from the first time I was fired. Being fired, to put it simply, sucks.

Larry King, Lee Iacocca, Michael Bloomberg, Muhammad Ali, Jesse Ventura, and Bernie Marcus have at least three things in common: They are all Business Superheroes, they have all been fired, they have all actually been better for it—at least according to Harvey MacKay's book *We Got Fired! . . . And It's the Best Thing That Ever Happened to Us*. But even without reading that book, we all know the words of consolation offered to those who are fired: "Don't worry," "It was meant to be," or "Remember that when one door closes, another opens." I too heard those words; I'd even heard that being fired could be a good thing if only you turn it into one. Nevertheless, the first time I was fired, it . . . sucked.*

However, once I got over feeling the pain, I was able to start to look at the alternatives that opened up for me precisely because of the firing. So yes, the firing was an external force that did affect me, but it was *I* who chose what came next. (I chose an eight-week European vacation, which I highly recommend upon being fired.)

*Actually, to be accurate, after my internship as a young corporate lawyer, my firm simply chose not to renew my employment contract, on the basis that I "wasn't worth the investment" because they believed (correctly, as it turns out) that I wouldn't practice law for long.

THE SILVER SURFER: OUTWIT ULTIMATUMS

In 1966, as their creation the *Fantastic Four* approached landmark issue #50, Stan Lee and Jack Kirby, the men behind the resurgence of comics in America, introduced two characters that remain staples of the Marvel universe to this very day. The first was the 100-foot-tall Devourer of Worlds, Galactus. The second was his herald, the Sentinel of the Spaceways, the Silver Surfer.

WHO IS THE SILVER SURFER?

Within two years, the Silver Surfer had such a large following that fans demanded more page space for him than his occasional appearances in *Fantastic Four* would allow, so in August 1968 the Marvel House of Ideas gave fans what they wanted: A new ongoing series, which kicked off with *The Origin of the Silver Surfer*.

Before his transformation into the Silver Surfer, astronomer Norrin Radd learned that his planet, Zenn-La, was scheduled for destruction by the gigantic Galactus, Devourer of Worlds. Radd ensured his planet's protection by offering to serve as Galactus's herald, responsible for traveling throughout galaxies on a spaceship that resembles a surfboard, in search of new planets for the Devourer of Worlds to consume. In order to enable him to perform this task, he was given a tiny amount of Galactus's Power Cosmic, which gave the Surfer his distinctive silvery skin and his ability to manipulate energy and matter.

The Surfer entered the comic universe as a consequence of his encounter with the Fantastic Four (a superhero team discussed further in Chapter 25), when Earth had been targeted for destruction. As Norrin Radd had previously dissuaded Galactus from destroying Zenn-La, the Fantastic Four similarly convinced the Silver Surfer to stop facilitating the destruction of innocent life. Earth thus became the second planet saved from destruction

at the hands of Galactus by the Silver Surfer, who was punished for his betrayal by suffering exile there.

WHY DOES THE SILVER SURFER MATTER?

The Silver Surfer is one of the most recognizable characters among fans of comics and pop culture. He has inspired a multitude of albums, most notably 1989's *Surfing with the Alien*, by Joe Satriani. He has also starred in both a Saturday-morning cartoon and the second Fantastic Four movie.

However, the real relevance of the Surfer was designed by his creator, Lee, who established the character as the voice for a generation of disenfranchised youth who valued moral principles more than received authority. Lee often used the Surfer's alienation on Earth to give him a unique vantage point from which to pontificate on the sorry state of the planet—a vibe that many readers in the late 1960s were digging.

LESSON 1 What Can You Learn from the Silver Surfer?

Lesson: Don't Buy into Ultimatums

In the *Fantastic Four*, Galactus is introduced as the Devourer of Worlds, a being so powerful that he needs to consume the life energy of living planets to survive. When the origin tale of the Silver Surfer begins, the Surfer's home world is next on the behemoth's dinner list. In fact, the residents of the Surfer's planet are powerless to stop Galactus and thus resign themselves to destruction; Norrin Radd is less quick to surrender, and both his world's survival and his new identity are the result of his ability to recognize opportunities that neither his countrymen nor their enemy were able to imagine.

For Business Superheroes, the true moral of the Surfer's story comes from his dealing with his one-time master, Galactus. Both when he saves his own planet and, later, when he saves the Earth, the Surfer refuses to buy into set thinking ("The planet is doomed, and I can't do anything to help"). He instead looks within for creative solutions, relying on out-of-the-box thinking to resolve the matter favorably. The same technique is vital for Business Superheroes.

Years ago, I was the leader of a group of employees at Ernst & Young. One day, my bosses decided to shut down my business unit and instructed me to lay off the entire staff. This, of course, didn't sit well with me: I had handpicked each member of the team and hired each away from a well-paying job. Further, this layoff was due to a change in the firm's strategy rather than any failure to deliver on the part of my team. After giving it much thought, I returned to my bosses and informed them that I wasn't prepared to fire anyone. Instead, I asked for ninety days, to try to place each member of the team in a new position, either inside the firm or with clients. I was successful in the end, and all members of the team found new work, with no disruption to their economic stability. No less significant, the firm was spared the considerable expense of the severance packages that laying off the employees would have entailed. So, by not blindly following orders, by not buying into set thinking, I was able to create a situation in which everyone benefited.

The real key to this lesson, like that of so many of the lessons we can learn from superheroes, is that applying these tricks is 5 percent inspiration and 95 percent perspiration. Meaning that, once you know what you need to do (in Silver Surfer's case, creating a new, third alternative), success is a matter of finding such alternatives consistently.

THE HULK: KEEP YOUR COOL

"Don't make me angry. You wouldn't like me when I'm angry." Those are the words most people associate with the Incredible Hulk, although most probably remember the words because of the TV series starring Bill Bixby and Lou Ferrigno as, respectively, Bruce Banner and his green-skinned alter ego, rather than the comic book series on which it was based.

WHO IS THE HULK?

The year was 1962, Stan Lee's *Fantastic Four* was selling like hotcakes, and it was time for the House of Ideas (that is, Marvel Comics) to debut its second hero.

Continuing on with their guiding belief that heroes should be flawed, Lee and Jack Kirby reenvisioned Robert Louis Stevenson's novella *The Strange Case of Dr. Jekyll and Mr. Hyde*. This version saw Dr. Bruce Banner become irradiated with gamma rays, which caused the meek, mild physicist's transformation (when angered) into a seven-foot-tall man-monster called the Hulk.

The premise, which hasn't radically changed in more than forty years, highlights the conflict between Banner and his self-inflicted curse: His alter ego, the Incredible Hulk. Banner is a feeble genius; the Hulk is a behemoth with the mind of a child. Banner has no physical presence; the Hulk is infinitely strong, can leap miles in the air, and has virtually impenetrable skin.

WHY DOES THE HULK MATTER?

Like Dr. Jekyll's famous alternate personality, the Hulk has been explained as the manifestation of a scientist's suppressed psyche. This fact has been borne out by the many and varied transformations experienced by other characters who were similarly exposed to gamma rays. In each case, the transformation forces some hidden part of the subject's psyche to emerge. For example, the Leader (the Hulk's arch-nemesis) is transformed from an average Joe into the superintelligent despot.

Which really brings up the question: What does *your* psyche hold? After all, even Business Superheroes have issues. The key is how we deal with them. Will you allow them to ruin your life (as they did Banner's) or will you master them to further your own goals (as the Leader did)?

LESSON 1 What Can You Learn from The Hulk?

Lesson: Don't Get Angry

Have you ever had a boss who thought that shouting at employees was a source of motivation? How do you think that works as a long-term strategy? Let me tell you—it doesn't work well.

The best leaders (and Business Superheroes) are able to channel their feelings into more positive outcomes. In fact, that principle doesn't apply just to anger but also to frustration and other negative emotions. The important thing is keeping control of how you demonstrate them. It's okay to be mad at customers, teammates, or employees, but before you choose to share that negativity with others, first examine the purpose you expect the confrontation to serve. If, in the end, all that will be accomplished is your venting and their feeling resentful, think twice.

My personal benchmark is to wait a night before sharing my feelings on a matter, and even then I share only if there is a strategic purpose for doing so.

THE HULK OF THE REAL WORLD

Norman Di Pasquale is my choice for the Hulk of the real world. Which of course begs the question, Who is Norman Di Pasquale?

Norm is the founder of En Vogue Computers, a high-tech consulting firm that acts as a cost-effective outsourced IT department for many leading firms, including mine. And if there is one thing that can lead to Hulk-like anger in the modern business world, it is broken computers.

In the twenty-first century, we expect our computers to run like "dial-tone technology" (a term that attests to the reliability of our telephones to provide a dial tone virtually every time we pick them up). We all know, however, that such reliability simply is not the case for computer systems and networks. Computers do many things today, including causing frustration when they don't work when and how we need them to. Norm and his team fix such problems.

But what has always amazed me about Norm isn't his ability to fix almost anything computer related; it's his uncanny ability to avoid getting angry or frustrated, no matter the circumstances. Norm has fixed the same issue multiple times for me, and somehow he always does it with a smile. Norm has been forced to tackle some ridiculously complex or unreasonable issues, yet never loses his good humor. Most of all, Norm has dealt with clients who are freaking out over their computer's downtime, yet it never seems to rattle him. Is it because he will turn into a giant green Goliath if he allows the issue at hand to aggravate him? I suspect not. It is more probably because Norm knows that keeping a level head when others around you lose theirs is a superpower unto itself—one that facilitates addressing issues efficiently. And that's good for business.

WONDER WOMAN: STAY FOCUSED

Lynda Carter will forever go down in history for her rare feat of enabling a female superhero to make an impact on young boys everywhere. In 1975, the Amazon warrior princess debuted on television, with Carter in the leading role. This was many people's first introduction to the character, even though she had been published by DC Comics continuously since the early 1940s.

WHO IS WONDER WOMAN?

Alongside Batman and Superman, Wonder Woman forms the third hero in DC's Big Three and has become the role model for many heroes (and comic book readers). Born to the queen of the Amazons on Paradise Island, the warrior princess Diana bested her fellow Amazon tribe mates in combat to win the role as Amazonian ambassador to Man's World. What is even more interesting than the Wonder Woman myth, however, is the legend of her creator, William Moulton Marston.

Marston was the inventor of the polygraph (lie detector machine); he was also a psychologist who lived in a polyamorous relationship and espoused other alternative sexual practices. He created Wonder Woman at the urging of his wife, Elizabeth Holloway Marston. According to an interview with Olive Byrne (Marston's lover, who lived with the married couple), Elizabeth asked him to create a character who would show that right can triumph over might and that one can be a pacifist as well as a warrior. No doubt influenced by these ideas, early Wonder Woman stories featured a superhero armed with a Lasso of Truth and Amazonian Bracelets of Submission. The plots were organized around titillating scenes of women tied and gagged, punctuated by speeches defending the appropriateness of Fighting for Peace.

WHY DOES WONDER WOMAN MATTER?

Before Wonder Woman's arrival during the Golden Age of Comics, women in comic books were relegated to roles as love interests and plot foils. Wonder Woman turned this notion on its head and was even tasked with rescuing army intelligence officer Steve Trevor and other men. She also became the role model for comic book femmes fatales in decades to come, including Ms. Marvel, She-Hulk, Black Canary, and the Wasp.

LESSON 1 What Can You Learn from Wonder Woman?

Lesson: Have a Mission

Few superheroes have been analyzed as extensively as Wonder Woman, largely because of debates among feminist theorists over her authenticity as a figure of female empowerment. (Three years before the television show aired, this debate entered the mass media. Wonder Woman was the subject of a 1972 cover story for *Ms.* magazine, which was then edited by Gloria Steinem.) Leaving that controversy aside, let's look at what Wonder Woman teaches Business Superheroes.

Remember Golden Rule 2: Swear an oath. Superheroes need a purpose, something to focus on and strive for. The same is true for Business Superheroes. Wonder Woman's purpose, or mission, is to "Fight for Peace" and to lead by example. What's yours? To find out, take a moment to review the oath you created for "Superhero Exercise: Crafting an Oath" (page 10) and see if you can determine the deeper mission that lies behind it. Because a Business Superhero's oath is often a statement of strategy, that strategy can be adopted most effectively when you understand how it applies to the context of your deeper mission. Superheroes focus their work efforts on their purpose, or mission, and the question of your own targeted mission will arise again in Chapter 20, when I ask you to determine your niche by first exploring the thing you are most passionate about. So take a moment to consider that passion now.

For me, the idea of having a clearly defined mission to direct my focus has been extremely helpful. By articulating my firm's mission ("To bridge the gap between entrepreneurs and equity") early on, I was able to help Wise Mentor Capital create the clean, consistent messaging that is so vital to establishing a brand. (One example of this is our tagline, "Wise Counsel for Smart Companies," which was designed to be consistent with and inspire confidence in our mission.) Just as important, a clearly defined articulation of our mission helped us determine priorities by ensuring that our focus stayed narrow (see Chapter 34 to understand why you can't be all things to all people). Your mission is really what you stand for, and standing for something is an important key to success.

The Big Moo is a book written collaboratively by "The Group of 33" (a collective of thirty-three cutting-edge business thinkers and business authors) and edited by Seth Godin, one of the group's members. In it, the authors repeatedly emphasize the importance of standing for something. In the aptly titled chapter "What Do You Stand For?" they show how Rockport shoes truly achieved broad success only when the company's original purpose (making great shoes for walking) evolved into a more general mission of helping people maintain their health. This clearer sense of purpose helped the company tap into Americans' needs, as the population began adopting the principles of not smoking, eating properly, and exercising (especially walking) in the 1980s. This in turn permitted Rockport to clearly understand and communicate the value of its products to prospective customers. The company was also able to complete its branding by developing health resources that supported its newly defined mission, including the Rockport Fitness Test and the Rockport Walking Diet. In response, the customers confirmed Rockport's value: The company garnered over $200 million in revenue in less than five years.

Guy Kawasaki, another member of The Group of 33, talks extensively about the need to create a mission in his must-read book *The Art of the Start*. In the very first chapter, Kawasaki begs readers to focus on "making meaning," rather than simply making money. He argues that if you treat your company as simply another commodity to be invested in and sold for profit, "you're doomed." Instead, he says, great companies become great precisely because they are focused on purposes beyond profits. After all, a company that exists simply for the sake of profit is like an employee who works simply for a paycheck, and the consequences are likely to be low-quality products that are easily expendable. On the other hand, companies motivated by a mission interpret their profits as proof that they are effectively fulfilling that mission and as external validation of their value.

So just like Wonder Woman (and the most successful business leaders of our time), craft a mission that you want to be your mantra.

BLACK BOLT: SILENCE IS GOLDEN

With a word, his voice can shatter steel and concrete. He is the king of a secret society, hidden away from humanity for millions of years. He is Black Bolt, ruler of the Inhumans.

WHO IS BLACK BOLT?

Black Bolt is the head of the royal family of a secret offshoot of humanity called the Inhumans. The group was created millions of years ago when aliens manipulated the genes of *Homo sapiens* to create a new being. Each Inhuman is exposed at birth to the mysterious mutagen, Terrigen Mist, which leads to radical physiological changes and often results in superpowers.

Black Bolt and the Inhumans have been a consistent element in the Fantastic Four series since their debut in *Fantastic Four* #45. Black Bolt's cousin Crystal joined the Fantastic Four as a replacement during Invisible Woman's maternity leave.

Like all members of the Inhuman society, Black Bolt was exposed to Terrigen Mist.* In his case, the physiological change was seemingly minor: His vocal cords mutated, granting him a supersonic voice. However, his power came at a cost; Black Bolt can't fully control his voice, so even the slightest whisper can level a city the size of New York. Consequently, Black Bolt is known for the silence that he has rigorously cultivated to control the effects of his power.

WHY DOES BLACK BOLT MATTER?

Contrary to what my mother thinks, she is *not* the originator of the maxim "We have two ears and one mouth so that we can listen twice as much as we speak." Although she enjoys citing this to me regularly (and perhaps I deserve it), the quote is said to date back to the Greek philosopher Epictetus, around 100 CE.

The saying instructs us to listen more than we talk—something that many people struggle with. The benefit of this advice is simple: Active listening is the key to building healthy relationships with others, while demonstrating respect for those to whom you are listening.

It is not enough to simply *hear* people; you need to *listen* to

*The Inhumans undertook the practice of deliberate genetic manipulation to maintain genetic variation within their population. Because there are only a few thousand Inhumans, they would otherwise suffer the effects of inbreeding.

them. Not just with your ears, but with your attention, your body, your whole self. By doing this, you will leave speakers with the sense that you deeply respect what they have to say. You do not have to believe what others tell you, but if you don't listen carefully in the first place, you lose an opportunity to learn.

LESSON 1 What Can You Learn from Black Bolt?

Lesson: Active Listening

According to multiple books on the topic of communication, humans spend close to 80 percent of their waking hours communicating—more specifically, doing one of four things: speaking, listening, reading, or writing. About half that time is spent absorbing information, and the other half is spent disseminating information. Although we received formal instruction in reading and writing, most of us received no instruction in listening.

Here are some tips to help you become a more effective listener. Try to meet these goals for two weeks and see the impact they have on both your relationships and your business results.

- **Stop talking.** Especially about yourself. It is human nature that our favorite topic is ourselves. But that applies no less to the person with whom you're speaking, so give people the floor and allow them to talk, especially about themselves—they might welcome your interest.

- ★ **Look at the person.** Focus your entire body on the speaker. Remember that a large portion of our interpersonal communication is nonverbal, so it is important to match your body language to your intent.
- ★ **Don't multitask while listening.** Suspend other things you are doing because it is physically impossible to listen at a high level while doing a second activity.
- ★ **Pay attention to feelings.** Remember that humans are emotional beings, and they convey those feelings not just with words but also through nonverbal communication.
- ★ **Be interested, not interesting.** Be sincerely interested in what the other person is talking about. No matter the topic, if you try hard enough, you can find something to be interested in. Developing the imaginative skills to appreciate topics that you hadn't previously thought about is an integral step in looking for and taking advantage of opportunities (see Chapter 9).
- ★ **Restate what the person said.** This is both a test of your listening and synthesizing skills and an invitation for the speaker to elaborate on specific points.
- ★ **Ask lots of questions.**
- ★ **Prompt the other person to continue.** Make sure your responses encourage the speaker; don't simply stand by, waiting for your turn to begin.

Active listening is hard, especially for Business Superheroes, who tend to have much to discuss and many interesting things on their minds. However, active listening is powerful strategically.

LESSON 2 What Can You Learn from Black Bolt?

Lesson: The Value of Silence

Black Bolt teaches us the value of silence. We talk way more than we need to and, therefore, often disclose way more than we should. Explore the following to see just how little we need to speak:

- **Silence and negotiation.** When you play poker, do you keep your cards close to your chest or lay them on the table for all to see? If you don't show your hand, you keep all your options open (no one knows the cards you are holding, so you can fold, bet, or call for another card). The same is true in business. Why tell others your opinion before learning theirs? If you hear their opinion first, you can keep all your options open (you can agree, disagree, or say nothing). On the other hand, if you lead with your opinion, you have nowhere to go because you have already shown your hand.
- **Silence and goals.** Be discreet when disclosing your own goals. Although articulating a goal can help you to visualize it and in turn achieve it (see Chapter 3),

SUPERHERO EXERCISE 8

The Monk

To see the true value of silence, avoid speaking for one full day. Unless directly asked something, don't speak. Don't share your opinion. Don't respond to things that don't require a response. Don't engage in idle chitchat. Try this for twenty-four hours, and you will see the true value of silence and realize how much of the speech we engage in daily is, in fact, superfluous.

there is seldom an upside to disclosing your goal to others. After all, if you fail to hit your intended target, no one will know, unless you have told him or her in advance. Obviously, you can't hide all your goals; revealing sales quotas will help guide your team. But if your goal is to be CEO within ten years, you may want to be discreet when choosing with whom you share such information.

* **Silence and self-promotion.** Don't publicize your successes too widely. I believe success speaks for itself; blowing your own horn is unnecessary.
* **Silence and action.** Finally, I advise the CEOs of my companies to "walk softly and carry a big stick," when it comes to leadership. I never recommend making threats, especially in regard to employee discipline.

Instead I suggest that the CEO lay out the issue at hand, firmly and quietly, giving the person in question a chance to reform. However, if the team member isn't able to rectify the situation, I recommend swift action, including immediate termination when necessary. Nothing is gained by screaming at employees and then letting them continue.

WOLVERINE: STRIVE FOR EXCELLENCE

"I'm the best there is at what I do, but what I do isn't very nice." One of the most famous lines in comics belongs to none other than Canada's own pint-size, claw-wielding mutant: Wolverine. Since his arrival in 1974, Wolverine has become the bruiser of the X-Men, the Batman of the Marvel universe, and one of the greatest stars of the Silver Age of Comics. In 2009, Wolverine will even get his own solo movie. Not bad for a guy who stands barely five feet three inches.

WHO IS WOLVERINE?

The question of who is Wolverine plagued comic fans for over twenty years after his introduction in *Incredible Hulk* #180. Created by Len Wein and John Romita Sr. as a throwaway antagonist for the Hulk, Wolverine truly blossomed under Chris Claremont and Frank Miller's penmanship—the former drew Wolverine during his legendary X-Men run, whereas the latter illustrated the claw-wielding madman's self-titled limited series. In fact it was in that very series that Miller coined Wolverine's menacing job-description, quoted at the beginning of this chapter.

Only recently has Wolverine's history been revealed. This diminutive pugilist is a mutant with a healing factor so powerful it actually slows his aging (similar to Adam on NBC's *Heroes*) and grants him heightened senses and reflexes. Wolverine's healing ability allowed him to survive the process of having adamantine (the hardest known metal in the Marvel universe) injected into his bones and three-foot-long claws surgically implanted in his forearms.

Wolverine's strengths include his razor-sharp claws (which are capable of cutting through anything), unbreakable bones, animal senses, and a healing factor that can recover from almost any wound. It isn't hard to see why the Canadian government attempted to turn James "Logan" Howlett into an unstoppable warrior.

WHY DOES WOLVERINE MATTER?

In his 2007 bestseller *The Dip*, Seth Godin, a real-world Business Superhero, goes into great detail to show readers why it pays to be number one. Godin shares his adaptation of Zipf's law, stating:

"The rewards [of success] are heavily skewed, so much so that it's typical for #1 to get ten times the benefit of #10, and a hundred times the benefit of #100."

Godin proves this throughout the first chapters of his book, teaching us that being the best in the world is seriously underrated.

LESSON 1 What Can You Learn from Wolverine?

Lesson: Be the Best at What You Do

Winners win big because the marketplace loves a winner, regardless of whether we're talking about college applications or movie ticket sales. Consequently, if you want to be a Business Superhero then you need to follow Wolverine's motto and be the best at what you do.

Now you may be asking yourself, "Self, I'm a middle manager, one of hundreds at this company. Does this really apply to me?" The answer is yes, Yes, YES! Whether you are the director of first impressions (the receptionist) or the leader of the bookkeepers (CFO), dedicating yourself to being the best is the first step to becoming a Business Superhero.

As I discuss in Chapter 16, Jack Welch is one of my favorite Business Superheroes. When I met with Welch a few years ago, I was fascinated by his "6 or 9" theory. According to Welch, who helped make General Electric (GE) one of the most powerful companies in the world, all employees can be divided and ranked as either 6s (out of 10) or 9s (out of 10). To Welch, 6s are worthless and take up precious resources (money, time, management focus); 9s are gold and need to be developed, nurtured, and mined for value. Welch applied this ranking methodology to everyone at GE, including receptionists, middle managers, and even suppliers. So ask yourself if you want to be 6 or a 9. Obviously, if only to keep your job, you want to be a 9. You want to be someone who excels and is invaluable.

But even if your boss is less rigid than Welch, there is still value to striving to be the best. I estimate that a typical adult spends more than half of his or her waking hours either at work or thinking about work. A life that is half devoted to something that you're not passionate about is, actually, a life half lived. No less important, because you are focused at work why not focus on being the best? After all, the old maxim remains true today: Anything worth doing is worth doing well.

IRON MAN: THE NEED FOR CONTINUOUS IMPROVEMENT

In what may go down as a brilliant act of ironic casting, Robert Downey Jr., who has become known for his long-standing battles with alcohol and substance abuse and has been reportedly in and out of rehab over the last decade, donned the gold and crimson armor of Iron Man in 2008. Why is that ironic? Because in the comics (and film) the man behind the suit, billionaire industrialist Tony Stark, is the original alcoholic superhero. In fact, in the historic *Iron Man* #170, Tony is forced to give up superherodom while he recovers from his addiction (just as Downey was once forced to put his acting career on hold).

WHO IS IRON MAN?

Created as a collaborative effort by Stan Lee, Larry Lieber (Lee's younger brother), Don Heck, and Jack Kirby, Iron Man first appeared in Marvel's 1963 *Tales of Suspense* #39. Like so many of

Marvel's Silver Age protagonists, Iron Man's alter ego is deeply flawed and struggles with his internal demons little less than with his supervillain opponents. Although the story of Iron Man's origin has been subject to repeated revision, all versions basically follow the same general premise:

- ★ Billionaire industrialist Tony Stark makes his money selling weapons to the U.S. military.
- ★ Stark observes the performance of his products in a foreign theater of combat (originally Vietnam, then China, and more recently Afghanistan).
- ★ During the observation, Stark is captured by the enemy, who demand that he build them a weapon of mass destruction.
- ★ Stark is injured during the capture, and a piece of shrapnel gets lodged in his chest, edging close to his heart and threatening to kill him.
- ★ Unwilling to build weapons for the enemy and desperately wishing to survive, Stark builds a rudimentary suit of armor, which he uses not only to escape imprisonment but also to save his life.
- ★ Stark returns to America, refines the armor, and decides to devote his life to using his technology to protect the innocent, taking on the Iron Man persona.

WHY DOES IRON MAN MATTER?

Before Marvel ushered in the Silver Age, comics were strictly one-dimensional. Heroes were good and did good; villains were vile and did evil. Lee's work on Iron Man and the likes of Spider-Man, the Hulk, and the Fantastic Four drove comics to new levels, forcing readers to explore the compelling issues of the day.

In the case of Iron Man, the hot issue on the mind of readers, according to Lee's account, was the role of the military-industrial complex in America. Stark's persona as an inventor, industrialist, playboy, and eccentric bears a striking resemblance to the iconic Howard Hughes, and the two also share a passionate anticommunist philosophy. Throughout Iron Man's comic run, recurring themes concerning technology—particularly its role in America's defense—are revisited. Later, as America moved past the cold war, Iron Man's conflicts evolved from his fight against communism into his more personal battle against his addiction.

Besides continuing to show the depth to which comics can treat socially relevant issues, Iron Man demonstrates the value of continual improvement, with Tony Stark (and the illustrators at Marvel) frequently upgrading his battle suit's look and feel.

LESSON 1 What Can You Learn from Iron Man?

Lesson: Pursue Lifelong Learning and Continual Improvement

One of the greatest lessons an up-and-coming Business Superhero can learn is that lifelong learning is necessary, regardless of the success you have had to date. When Tony Stark first creates his armor, it is depicted as the most advanced technology in the world, yet the first thing Stark does after returning to the United States is totally revamp his battle suit, a process of improvement that continues to this day, despite Stark's unthreatened status as the foremost technologist in the Marvel universe.

Similarly, bestselling author Dennis Waitley espouses the need for lifelong learning in his 1988 book, *The Seeds of Greatness*, in which he instructs us to "View life as a continuous learning experience."

Continual improvement is one of the key tactics cited by many CEOs, including Home Depot founders Arthur Blank and Bernie Marcus, who created their $90 billion hardware empire by focusing on that concept. In their tell-all book *Built from Scratch*, the pair credits much of their success to their efforts to improve something at each of their stores, each and every day. Marcus, who served as company CEO for the first nineteen years, urges managers to "never be satisfied with how things are done" and to always seek to improve and reinvent processes, ranging from customer service to warehouse inventory control.

IRON MAN OF THE REAL WORLD

As I noted earlier, Jack Welch, who is often called the best CEO of the late twentieth century, is credited with transforming General Electric into the world's most valuable company. He takes Waitley's proposition of lifelong learning to the next level, stating: "An organization's ability to learn, and translate that learning into action rapidly, is the ultimate competitive advantage."

Welch's latest book (cowritten with his wife, Suzy), *Winning: The Answers: Confronting 74 of the Toughest Questions in Business Today*, develops this point further: "It is the continuous, aggressive improvement of what you already sell or how you already do business. Companies can (and must!) also innovate by searching for best practices, adapting them, and continuously improving them. . . . The process of continuous improvement really has no boundaries or limits."

Continuous improvement is not only a policy that Welch believes in strongly, it is a policy that he is world renowned for implementing ruthlessly. He earned the nickname "Neutron Jack" during the early 1980s. Every year he would fire the bottom 10 percent of GE's staff, which consequently went from 411,000 employees in 1980 to 299,000 in 1985. That's a reduction of 112,000 employees (or 27 percent) over a five-year period. When I asked him in 2002 how he felt about being compared to a neutron bomb (which is said to kill living things while leaving infrastructure intact), he shot back: "If you want your garden to grow, you need to cultivate the flowers and pull the weeds."

SPIDER-MAN: WITH GREAT POWER COMES GREAT RESPONSIBILITY

"Spider-Man, Spider-Man, does whatever a spider can. Spins a web, any size, catches thieves just like flies. Look Out! Here comes the Spider-Man." Those are the unforgettable lyrics from the theme song of the 1967 *Spider-Man* cartoon series based on the comic. The cartoon was so cheaply produced that they didn't even bother to draw in the webbing on Spidey's costume, other than the head, feet, and arms. So cheap that they consistently reused stock footage (I mean, he swings by the same building five or six times in a row in the opening sequence alone). So cheap that the spider on the costume's front and back mistakenly had only six legs but continued to be used for all of season one—even after the error was identified. But in the forty years since then our wall-crawling protagonist has come a long way; the third Spider-Man movie is rumored to have cost, all in, almost $500 million to make and promote.

WHO IS SPIDER-MAN?

Spider-Man is one of the world's most recognized icons. Created by Stan Lee and Steve Ditko in 1962, Spider-Man set the new standard for complicated teenage heroes and selfless urban vigilantes. He also set a new standard with his ability to make one-line quips while fighting heinous villains.

Bitten by a radioactive spider (more recently described as a genetically altered radioactive spider), Peter Parker (Spidey's real name) originally used his newfound powers to garner fame and fortune as a TV star. Later, Peter's self-absorption prevents him from apprehending an escaping thief. When that thief goes on to kill Peter's beloved father figure, Uncle Ben, Peter learns that "With great power comes great responsibility." The death of Uncle Ben leads Peter to abandon his quest for fame and fortune and instead to dedicate himself to fighting injustice.

Peter's powers include possessing the proportional strength, reflexes, and speed of a spider. He has great agility and can cling to walls. Most important, of course, he can spin webs (a skill that the comic attributes to web-shooter technology and the movie attributes to his physical changes).

WHY DOES SPIDER-MAN MATTER?

As noted in the introduction, the exact source of Spider-Man's oath—"With great power comes great responsibility"—is unknown. Nevertheless, Spidey reminds Business Superheroes of the moral imperative to protect the innocent, defend the weak, and ensure that justice prevails.

LESSON 1 What Can You Learn from Spider-Man?
Lesson: Take Responsibility

It sounds trite to say that Business Superheroes need to take responsibility, but in our context I mean this in three separate but interrelated ways:

- ★ Take responsibility to share the credit and rewards.
- ★ Take responsibility for failure.
- ★ Take responsibility not to criticize, condemn, or complain.

Responsibility to Share

The primary interpretation of the Spider-Man axiom is that if you have power then you must use it responsibly. This topic has been explored in many other tomes at sufficient length. One need look only to Bono or Bill Gates to see demonstrations of the proper use of fame and fortune. However, I'm not sure future superheroes understand fully what's in it for them if they adhere to this principle.

Doing right by others not only makes you feel good, it generates good business karma (see Chapter 5) and often leads to a Business Superhero gaining more personal power (see Chapter 21).

Responsibility for Failure

Your boss gives you a deadline to produce a PowerPoint presentation for her use at next week's conference. Come deadline day, that presentation will either be done or not done—there's no third option. Does your boss really care that your kids were sick? Or that you had other priorities? Her conference date is approaching, and you either have the material ready or you don't. Some things in life are binary: The PowerPoint slides are either ready or not ready. All the reasons (however justified) in the world can explain the problem, but none will fix it.

My mother, Bev Wise, taught me a lot of things over the thirty-seven years she has known me (see Chapter 35). One of her most memorable pearls of wisdom is this: There are a thousand reasons not to get something done; only one to get something done. The one reason being, of course, that you committed to delivering on your promise; you didn't commit to delivering on your promise *only* if your kids weren't sick.

Business Superheroes should accept the fact that excuses (even valid explanations and mitigating factors) don't change the reality that some things in life are binary. If a document needs to be in New York City by noon on Friday, it doesn't matter if the delivery guy was in an accident—a Business Superhero should have sent it early enough to ensure delivery. The lesson is simple: Understand that some things are simply binary. They either happen or they do not. And in those cases, recognize that the best reasons, explanations, and justifications may introduce mitigating factors, but they can never overcome the plain hard truth of success and failure.

Avoiding the Three Cs

As I've mentioned a couple of times already, one of the oldest and most successful self-help books is *How to Win Friends and Influence People*, by Dale Carnegie. If you are in training to become a Business Superhero and you still haven't read it, you really should. I read it first at age thirteen and have tried to read it semiannually since.

Of the many pieces of advice Carnegie espouses is not to criticize, condemn, or complain. Sound easy? Try it for one day. For an entire day banish all criticisms of others. For an entire day don't complain about anything, no matter how awful it might be. In the beginning it will be nearly impossible, but give it a few days, and you will likely develop a sort of "spider sense" of your own, allowing you to preemptively filter any of the three Cs. The real key is to understand that nothing is gained by using the three Cs—any one of them simply fosters negativity and/or puts the person on the other end in an emotionally defensive posture, one that it will be hard for either of you to overcome. But, most important, the problem with the three Cs is that they make communication counterproductive, because they create a disjunction between what you intend to communicate and what your listener takes away from the conversation.

After all, people are emotional creatures, and when we receive criticism (no matter how well-intentioned), we tend to shut down communication by responding defensively, even to the point of resenting the criticizer. For this reason, criticism typically achieves an outcome that is precisely the opposite of the desired one, since it often elicits unnecessary hostility that can exacerbate the problem that the criticizer is trying to address, rather than resolving it.

Let's take a real-world example. When my fiancée, Allie, and I first moved in together, I had been a bachelor since law school, living alone, leaving my shoes by the front door like a teenager home from school. Now that I shared my home with someone else, you would think I would be open to making changes. But, of course, as a stubborn guy, I was not. Allie started out with the typical, "Honey, can you move your shoes?" But after a hundred or so "Honey can yous," she quickly turned to complaining ("Why don't you pick up after yourself?") and later to criticizing ("You never clean up after yourself!"). Now, those statements are all true. I can't dispute them. Nor can I dispute Allie's right to make them or even the reasonableness of her position. Truth be told, if I had a choice *I* wouldn't live with me. Notwithstanding, each time my future bride uttered a word about the shoes, my back would go up, and I'd dig my heels in. If Allie's goal was "No shoes at the front door" that wasn't the effect, and her strategy was leading to the unintended consequences of tension and defensiveness.

So what could Allie do? Well, first she would need to recognize that using any of the three Cs would fail to generate the outcome she was seeking. Then she would have to be willing (and sufficiently imaginative) to develop another approach, which is exactly what she did.

Allie, being a superhero in her own right, found an alternative solution. First, she turned the complaint of "You never put your shoes away" to a simple and future-oriented request ("Please put your shoes away"), and then she helped me understand how my misplaced shoes were affecting her—through a demonstration.

Every once in a while, Allie would leave shoes for me to find. In my office. On my pillow. These mysterious foot coverings would pop up everywhere. I soon learned how annoying it could be and decided that my shoes had a home (the closet), where they needed to stay more regularly, and thus the Case of the Wandering Shoes was solved.

The lesson of inspiring change in others without complaint or criticism is not limited just to my home. It is also true in my office, and in offices around the world. One example that comes to mind is the Case of the Late Intern.

I once had a summer student to supervise. No matter what

meeting, no matter what time, he would arrive five minutes late. I found this to be disrespectful to both the rest of the team (who arrived five or more minutes early) generally, and to myself specifically (who had invested a considerable amount of time preparing for meetings to ensure they were valuable to all). My first reaction was to scold him, to criticize him. Then I wanted to complain. Finally, I actually wanted to publicly condemn his tardiness (in the hope of ensuring the rest of the team knew the matter was being addressed). But instead of taking the easy path and going with one of the three Cs, I tried a different approach: I took him out for coffee.

During coffee, I asked him what his goals were. Eventually he told me he wanted to join our firm and then, one day, go out on his own. After taking a dramatic pause, I asked him three questions:

- What role he felt "respect" would play in achieving his goals
- What role he felt "instilling confidence in clients" would play in achieving his goals
- What role he felt "teamwork" would play in achieving his goals

Once he had replied to all three questions, I asked him what effects he thought that being late might have on his teammates' and clients' perception of his respect for them, and how in turn their perceptions of him might affect his future employment. He was never late again.

MADROX: SYNERGISTIC MULTITASKING

Ever needed to be in two places at the same time? Ever had so much to do that you wished there were more than one of you? Well, Jamie Madrox, the Multiple Man, doesn't have to wonder what it would be like to have a clone—he makes clones of himself daily.

WHO IS MADROX?

Jamie Madrox, the Multiple Man, first appeared in the 1975 *Giant Size Fantastic Four* #4. It was quickly revealed that Madrox has the power to create an unlimited number of duplicates of himself (called "dupes"). Each duplicate can act independently, while being linked to all others.

The character, while always a fan favorite, seemed unable to get off of the D-list, even after several stints with the X-Men.

However, in 2004, writer Peter David took the character to a whole new level in the four-issue miniseries titled *MadroX*. There, David establishes that Madrox sends duplicates of himself to the four corners of the earth—each to live its own life, gather its own unique skills, and gain individual experience. Madrox then later (sometime after many years) reintegrates the duplicates, gaining all of the knowledge, experiences, and skills that each has acquired. In this manner, Madrox has absorbed the firsthand experience of being a Shaolin monk, a spy, a private investigator, a priest, and even an Olympic gymnast.

WHY DOES MADROX MATTER?

When I was writing this book, I was also:

* Writing a column for a national newspaper
* Working on a number one TV show
* Teaching business at a university
* Running a large venture capital fund
* Lecturing across North America, two or three times a month

The one question I get asked more than any other is, "How do you do it? How do you have so many full-time jobs?" My secret (and the secret of every Business Superhero I know) is practice; I've written about this extensively, creating a theory I call the Double Dip.* For the purposes of this tome, however, let's call it . . . the Madrox Principle.

LESSON 1 What Can You Learn from Madrox?

Lesson: Reap the Most Rewards

The Madrox Principle is a business theory that illustrates how to maximize monetization (that's venture capital slang for "making as much money as possible") from every activity you undertake or, in plain English, it shows you how to build once, sell twice, and make money three times. At the heart of the technique is a willingness to look at all opportunities for gain from a single action, including opportunities that may not be readily apparent.

For instance, I wrote this book for publication and sale, but I will also use some of the material when asked to give a presentation (for which I will get paid again). So I am double dipping, in that I have created the content once, but monetized it twice. That is at the heart of the Madrox Principle: Synergize your activities so you can gain multiple benefits from each action. You see this happening all the time in business and entertain-

*Sean Wise, "The Double Dip: How to Build Once, Sell Twice and Make Money Three Times," *Toronto Globe and Mail*, December 13, 2005.

MADROX OF THE REAL WORLD

While I may be a candidate for Madrox in the real world, truth be told, I learned the Madrox Principle from reading about another great Business Superhero—the father of *Star Wars* himself, George Lucas.

If you haven't heard the urban legend behind *Star Wars*, it goes a little something like this: Lucas was a young hotshot director but was having trouble getting a studio to back his dream project—an epic along the lines of Flash Gordon meets the Seven Samurai. To attract the backing he needed, Lucas waived his up-front fees as director, keeping instead the licensing rights, which the studio felt were nearly worthless.

Thirty years after Lucas waived the $100,000 fee, his legendary empire of toys, figures, video games, and the like is estimated to be worth more than $3.5 billion. How did he do it? Simple. The Madrox Principle: Build once and monetize constantly.

ment. Today's stars have perfumes, record labels, and TV shows, allowing them to leverage their brand across multiple platforms to generate revenue from diverse streams.

So take a moment, list all the things that you do daily, weekly, and monthly. See if you can categorize them and then see the level of synergy among the categories. If the synergy is low, challenge yourself to find ways to create more benefit without creating more things to do.

JUSTICE LEAGUE: EVEN SUPERHEROES NEED HELP

Superhero teams have existed since the dawn of the Golden Age of Comics. Groups like the Justice Society and the Invaders set the foundation for disparate heroes with common goals to gather together and tackle greater threats than any one hero could overcome. However, no team does this as memorably as the Justice League of America, which counts within its ranks Superman, Batman, Wonder Woman, the Green Lantern, Flash, Aquaman, Atom, Hawkman, Zatanna, and Firestorm.

This behemoth of justice has thrilled readers since its debut in 1960 in *The Brave and the Bold* #28, and continues to do so almost fifty years later, as the animated *Justice League* cartoon exposes a whole new generation to these super friends.

WHAT IS THE JUSTICE LEAGUE?

The Justice League is DC Comics' enduring pantheon of powerhouse characters. Their ranks include the Magnificent Seven (Superman, Batman, Wonder Woman, Flash, the Green Lantern, Aquaman, and the Martian Manhunter) as well as an ever-changing roster of heroes including the likes of:

- Doctor Fate
- Zatanna
- Hawkman
- Green Arrow
- Black Canary
- Steel
- Fire
- Ice
- Rocket Reds
- Blue Beetle
- Booster Gold
- Mister Miracle

Over time, the league has gone through several incarnations, even obtaining full-nation status at the United Nations for a short time.

WHY DOES THE JUSTICE LEAGUE MATTER?

Superman, Wonder Woman, and the Green Lantern are all omega-level powerhouses, each of whom is capable of overcoming almost anything his or her adversaries can dish out, yet each knows the benefit of teamwork and the power that a strong peer group can provide. So, while you may be on your way to being a Business Superhero in your own right, keep foremost in mind the value of teammates.

LESSON 1 What Can You Learn from the Justice League?
Lesson: Life Is a Team Sport

Nineteenth-century steel industrialist Andrew Carnegie, a Business Superhero if there ever was one, knew the power of a team: "Teamwork is the ability to work together toward a common vision. It is the fuel that allows common people to attain uncommon results." So if you want uncommon results, recognize that business, like life, is a team sport, requiring a group effort. Many successful people have already mastered this lesson.

Have you ever seen a director who received an Oscar go on stage and say, "This was all me"? How about a baseball player after winning the World Series? Don't they all have many team members to thank? So why should it be different in business?

Business Superheroes should heed this advice: Share the credit, hog the blame.

LESSON 2 What Can You Learn from the Justice League?

Lesson: Role Players Do Just That

I often wondered if Aquaman felt inadequate. Yes, I know that he was the king of the Seven Seas, and yes, I know that three-quarters of our planet's surface is covered by water, but c'mon. How many world (let alone intergalactic) crises require the use of sea creatures? So I wondered if he felt bad. I wonder if he felt like less of a super friend.

Then one day, I met Pat. While I was with Ernst & Young, Pat was my right-hand person. She started off as my secretary, but by the time I left she was a vital and necessary part of my team. In fact, she was the lynchpin.

Pat looked after all the details so I didn't have to. Her work allowed me to focus on the more strategic tasks at hand. Yes, it is true that photocopying seldom closes the big deal, but just try closing that deal with pages missing from your contracts . . . then you will know the power of the role player. That is the true power of Aquaman.

Aquaman, Green Arrow, and even the Elongated Man are just as important to the Justice League as the powerhouses Superman and the Green Lantern—just for different reasons. Similarly, the person who gets your mail, finalizes the contracts, or collects the invoice is as important as you are—just for different reasons. Business superheroes should heed the Aquaman Rule when recognizing the value of all members after a win. As basketball legend Michael Jordan said: "Talent wins games, but teamwork and intelligence wins championships."

So get some intelligence and recruit as good an Aquaman as you do a Wonder Woman.

GREEN ARROW: TARGET A NICHE

Batman with a bow. That's how I originally saw Green Arrow; it was only in later years that I realized the Emerald Archer was so much more than just a rip-off of Batman. As well as recognizing him as one of comics' most powerful voices in favor of social justice, I came to appreciate the fact that Green Arrow teaches Business Superheroes how to focus their attention on the one area that will make them great.

WHO IS GREEN ARROW?

Green Arrow first appeared in 1941 in the *More Fun Comics* anthology series. Many initially compared him (as I did) to an archery-inspired clone of Batman. (This judgment was not entirely unfounded—his alter-ego was billionaire industrialist Oliver Quinn, he ran around fighting crime with a teen sidekick, and he had an Arrowcar and even an Arrowcave.) Other readers saw Green Arrow as merely an updated version of Robin Hood—an allegory developed more explicitly in Green Arrow's later exploits, which focused on protecting the poor.

Still others saw the character as an imitation of Arrow, a character from Centaur Publications who debuted in 1938 and also used trick arrows to fight crime. No matter the inspiration for the character, Green Arrow is typically portrayed as a modern-day Robin Hood who defends the vulnerable using his quiver of trick arrows, including glue arrows, explosive arrows, grappling arrows, flash arrows, and the most famous of all the arrows in his arsenal—boxing glove arrows.

WHY DOES GREEN ARROW MATTER?

Although Green Arrow first appeared in 1941, he achieved significance and enduring popularity only twenty-five years later, when the billionaire Quinn lost his fortune. Like many other superheroes in both the comic world and the business one, he responded to this adversity with renewed conviction, and assumed a role more explicitly related to his predecessor Robin Hood, by becoming an inner-city champion of social justice.

Green Arrow's liberalism became explicitly contrasted with the conservatism of the Green Lantern when the two co-starred in a series during the 1970s, which became notable as one of the first comic book series to tackle social issues, ranging from inner-city decay to drug use to political corruption. There, the character found a voice and an identity that extended beyond novelty arrows and finally achieved enduring popularity among fans. In the ensuing years, the series has generally remained a gritty example of social realism in comics.

However, for Business Superheroes, the story of Green Arrow can be much more useful. In his international bestseller *Good to Great: Why Some Companies Make the Leap . . . and Others Don't*, Jim Collins introduces the Hedgehog Concept, which I believe nails the lesson that Green Arrow teaches us.

What is the Hedgehog Concept? Formulated by Collins, it advocates "a clear, focused understanding of what you can do better than anyone else in the world." Collins argues that a company can only go from being merely good (that is, profitable) to becoming great (that is, a world leader) by first determining what its focus should be. To help us figure out what our focus is, Collins reminds us of a quotation from the Greek poet Archilochus: "The fox knows many things, but the hedgehog knows one big thing." In other words, the fox can do many things adequately, but the hedgehog is adept at its specialty, on which it focuses exclusively. (If you want to know what that "one thing" is, read Collins's book. It will be well worth your time.)

LESSON 1 What Can You Learn from Green Arrow?

Lesson: Find Your Niche

The Hedgehog Principle applies to companies looking to go from good to great as well as to individuals looking to become Business Superheroes. While "foxes" pride themselves on their ability to multitask or to wear many different hats at the same time, tending to all of those unrelated activities can distract their attention and prevent them from focusing exclusively on the one or two things that they are capable of doing superbly. Green Arrow does one thing superbly: archery.

Collins directs us to three questions that help us to apply the Hedgehog Concept in the pursuit of excellence: What can we do better than anyone else? What are we passionate about? What specific single element drives our economic success? The nexus of these three areas (superiority, passion, and profit) is our "Hedgehog Zone." Business Superheroes need to learn from both the hedgehog and Green Arrow and focus on the thing they do better than others, the thing they are passionate about, and the thing that they can make money at.

CAPTAIN AMERICA: LEADERSHIP BEST PRACTICES

The Star-Spangled Avenger was created by Joe Simon and Jack Kirby in 1941 in an attempt to rally Americans against the rise of fascism in Nazi Germany before the United States was actively involved in the war. From the beginning, Captain America has stood for the very highest American ideals, even when those ideals were supported by neither the American government nor the majority of its population. Throughout his sixty-plus-year history, Captain America has repeatedly dramatized the conflict between principle and practice and has repeatedly had to resist his own government's attempts to pervert his legacy.

Most recently, American political strife in the Marvel universe became inflamed in the crossover *Civil War* series, which featured Captain America's open defiance of the conservative American government. When a terrorist event inspires the government to legislate restrictions on the civil rights of heroes through forced registration, Captain America leads the antiregistration opposition. Unfortunately, the civil war ends with the antiregistration forces losing the war and, worse yet, with Captain America's assassination.

WHO IS CAPTAIN AMERICA?

Before becoming Captain America, Steve Rogers was a sickly illustrator from New York, whose health kept him from joining the war effort overseas. Desperate to do his part, Rogers agreed to participate in Operation Rebirth, which sought to create American super-soldiers to fight the Nazis. Rogers was subjected to various tests to enhance his constitution, strength, speed, and reflexes and the formerly 4F army recruit was turned into America's perfect weapon.

Just moments after Rogers's transformation, however, the man behind Operation Rebirth was killed, leaving Rogers as the only working super-soldier created.

WHY DOES CAPTAIN AMERICA MATTER?

It is interesting to note that Captain America's beginnings are steeped in his creators' attempts to shine a light on fascism and, sixty years later, writer Ed Brubaker (who wrote Cap's death in *Captain America*, volume 5, #25) used the Sentinel of Liberty's death to once again shine a metaphorical light on contemporary events concerning government restrictions on civil liberties.

The superhero origins of Wolverine and Cap are closely related. Operation Rebirth was recently revealed to be part of a larger American government program known as Weapon Plus. Rogers, dubbed "Weapon One," is the first generation of living weapons of mass destruction created by the program. Years later, Wolverine (see Chapter 15) came into being as the tenth generation of Weapon Plus products, dubbed "Weapon X."

But Captain America's story is more than a simple allegory against fascism in all its forms. He provides the Business Superhero with several examples of leadership best practices, including:

- ★ Leading from the front
- ★ Being the brand
- ★ Not following orders blindly

LESSON 1 What Can You Learn from Captain America?

Lesson: Lead from the Front

When I was sixteen I served in Israel's Gadna (*Gedudei No'ar*). Gadna is the Youth Battalion run by Israel's ministry of defense—it's a sort of army cadets meets Boy Scouts, with real guns. It was here that I first learned about true leadership.

One of the fundamental principles that the Israel Defense Forces (IDF) taught in Gadna is "lead by example." Officers interpret this to mean that, in battle, leaders should lead from the front. The Israeli battle cry "*Aharai!*" means literally "after me."

After me may not have been his battle cry, but it sure was the essence of Captain America, who first led many a soldier into battle during World War II and later continued his battle-tested leadership in the field, as leader of Marvel's preeminent superteam, The Avengers.

The same can be true for Business Superheroes, who should never ask others to do something that they themselves aren't willing to do. You often hear this tenet espoused by leaders, particularly those who have worked their way up from the bottom, such as Jack Welch (see Chapter 16). When going into battle, Business Superheroes need to remember Captain America's example and inspire their teammates with the confidence and respect that true leadership commands.

LESSON 2 What Can You Learn from Captain America?
Lesson: Be Your Brand

Lead by example has a secondary meaning for both IDF soldiers and Captain America. Wearing an Israeli army uniform means that you are a representative of not just the army, but the state itself. Therefore, according to standing IDF orders, both soldiers and officers are expected to set a personal example.

Similarly, Business Superheroes should realize that they are their companies' brands externally and representatives of management internally. Their actions inevitably reflect on both the company and its leadership. As such, Business Superheroes should do their best to take actions and make statements that reflect well not only on themselves but on the company too.

So Business Superheroes need to "be the brand" both outside and inside the workplace. Keep this in mind as you communicate with others. Be your brand when meeting customers, leading a team meeting, or even sending an email. Keep at the forefront of your mind that you are a micro-representation of the greater organization; just as the DNA contained in a single cell can give us clues to the nature of the organism, your interactions with others reflect the culture of the company.

LESSON 3 What Can You Learn from Captain America?
Lesson: Rebel against Wrong

Being representatives of the company does not mean that Business Superheroes need to follow orders blindly. Just as Captain America did throughout his long career as the Star-Spangled Avenger, Business Superheroes are encouraged not to obey passively—they are required to think for themselves. Unwilling to lend his support to government policies that he felt transgressed the highest ideals of his country, Cap was willing to weather painful accusations of a lack of patriotism (and even treason) when his beliefs compelled him to dissent against those policies.

He was even willing to sacrifice the mantle of Captain America (fighting crime as the character Nomad instead) when he felt that the government was attempting to exploit that persona as a means of furthering policies that violated his (and America's) ideals. Needless to say, his brand was valuable to the government precisely because of the tremendous personal power that he had cultivated through decades of principled action in devotion to the very ideals that the administration asked him to abandon.

Similarly, Business Superheroes must recognize that their value to their organizations—whether as a brand or as a worker—must be rooted first and foremost in the integrity of their beliefs, words, and actions. By compromising their values, Business Superheroes compromise their value to all who depend on them.

ORACLE: BUILD A NETWORK

Before being shot in the spine, Barbara Gordon had defended the streets of Gotham City as Batgirl. Bound to a wheelchair after suffering a gunshot wound, Gordon took a new name and identity as Oracle, a go-to person for superheroes and law enforcement agents alike. Gordon combined her skills as a librarian and computer hacker with her knowledge of technology to become an expert online investigator for the superhero population.

WHO IS ORACLE?

In 1967, Commissioner Gordon's librarian niece, Barbara Gordon, donned a Batman-inspired costume and began her life as a costumed crime fighter. Like so many female superheroes from the Silver Age of Comics, Batgirl seemed originally to be nothing more than an attempt to increase readership by cloning a mainstay and making it female, like Supergirl, Aquagirl, and Hawkgirl. Indeed, given her lack of independence and originality, there was little at the beginning to suggest that her comics would leave any greater legacy than those of the other female clones.

That however all changed when writer Alan Moore ushered Barbara Gordon into the Dark Age of Comics by having the Joker shoot her in cold blood, in an attempt to drive her adopted father insane.

But paralysis was not to be the end of Barbara's crime-fighting exploits. Refusing retirement, Gordon traded in her batarangs for an intelligence network that would make the CIA jealous, and thus the information power broker Oracle was born.

Over the last decade Oracle has gone from being a secondary character—used mainly to progress story lines—to the center of her own comic series (titled *Birds of Prey*), in which she harnesses female agents to thwart all manner of evil uncovered by Gordon's detective skills. Her allies include the likes of Black Canary, Huntress, Big Barda, and the Martian Manhunter. Oracle also continues to act as the main information conduit for the likes of Nightwing, Batman, and the Justice League.

WHY DOES ORACLE MATTER?

A case could certainly be made that Oracle sets the bar for Golden Rule 10 (Overcoming adversity), as a superhero who remains undeterred by partial paralysis. But I think she really stands for much more than that. Over the last decade Oracle has shown the power of a strong network of contacts, and in doing so she shows Business Superheroes the importance of cultivating contacts and developing assets that can further their collective goals.

LESSON 1 What Can You Learn from Oracle?

Lesson: Cultivate Sources

In any intelligence community (like the CIA or MI5), handlers who act behind the scenes are only as good as the network of assets (who actually do the spying) they manage. Oracle shows the importance of building such a network. Business Superheroes should follow Oracle's lead and consciously pursue relationships both with sources of information (receptionists) and with agents in the field (members of the sales force). In doing so, the Business Superhero not only will be able to access critical information in a timely manner but also will be able to act on that information, if necessary. The easiest way to do that is to leverage natural law.

As described by Thomas Hobbes in his treatises *Leviathan* and *De Cive*, natural law is an all-encompassing foundational philosophical principle that states at its core: People will always do what is in their best interest and will avoid things that may cause them harm. Thus, if you want to get someone to do something for you (like share information, for example), you must always put yourself in the other person's shoes (see Chapter 4) to determine how that action might serve his or her best interests. By aligning your needs with your future agents' interests, you are more likely to get results and cultivate a successful, invaluable intelligence community.

DOCTOR STRANGE: NEVER TOO LATE TO CHANGE

"By the Hoary Hosts of Hoggoth!" Believe it or not, that is one of the incantations most often used by the Sorcerer Supreme of the Marvel Universe: Dr. Stephen Vincent Strange, known more colloquially as Doctor Strange.

WHO IS DOCTOR STRANGE?

Another creation of the stupendous Stan Lee (this time with artist Steve Ditko), Doctor Strange, like so many of his Marvel Silver Age compatriots, is a deeply flawed character. When his story opens, Strange is a world-renowned, but extremely arrogant, brain surgeon. Following a near-fatal automobile accident, Strange's loss of fine motor skills leaves him unable to perform surgery. Overwhelmed by the loss, Strange becomes depressed and later destitute, desperate to recover what he once took for granted. Having exhausted all conventional means to cure his condition, Strange journeys to the Himalayas in search of the Ancient One, who is rumored to have mystical cures far beyond those offered by the conventional Western medicine that Strange had practiced.

Strange discovers the Ancient One and foils a plot against the sorcerer's life, undertaken by Baron Mordo, the Ancient One's apprentice and Strange's future arch-nemesis. The Ancient One then adopts Strange as his new apprentice. At the end of his seven-year apprenticeship, Doctor Strange is ready to be both a selfless hero and a sorcerer supreme.

WHY DOES DOCTOR STRANGE MATTER?

Superheroes, even Business Superheroes, face challenges daily, challenges that they don't always overcome. Sometimes, we make the wrong decisions, follow the wrong path, or get involved with things we later regret. Doctor Strange shows that the power of redemption exists within us all, if only we choose to pursue it.

LESSON 1 What Can You Learn from Doctor Strange?

Lesson: Never Too Late

According to a Chinese proverb: The best time to plant a tree? Twenty years ago. The second best time to plant a tree? Today. Similarly, the best time to change your approach and return to actions that correspond to your highest principles is yesterday. The second best time is today. The keys of course are recognizing the mistake, committing to a change, and making that change. According to Jack Welch (profiled in Chapter 16), "mistakes can often be as good a teacher as success." Many times, all you need to do to get started is just commit to taking that first step on the path of change.

MR. FANTASTIC: BE FLEXIBLE

Reed Richards convinced his best friend, his fiancée, and his future brother-in-law to accompany him on an unauthorized trip into space. The trip led to all four being doused in cosmic radiation and gaining superpowers. Now, one can stretch like water, one can burn like flame, one is as transparent as the air, and one is as solid as rock. Together, they are the Fantastic Four, and since 1961 they have been the first family of the Marvel universe, led consistently by Reed Richards, Mr. Fantastic.

WHO IS MR. FANTASTIC?

The head of the Fantastic Four, Mr. Fantastic himself was named first on *Business Week*'s list of smartest superheroes ever. Richards is responsible for numerous breakthroughs and inventions in various scientific fields, including space travel, holography, and time travel. However his most notable invention is a technology called "unstable molecules." Used to make the fabric of a superhero's costume, the technology allows the costume to conform to the wearer's form and powers. It's particularly useful for Mr. Fantastic's own uniform, which doesn't rip when he stretches his body but instead adjusts to his elongated shape.

WHY DOES MR. FANTASTIC MATTER?

While Richards's marriage to Susan Storm (aka the Invisible Woman) was the first comic book marriage of two superheroes, Business Superheroes can learn much more from Mr. Fantastic than lessons in marital bliss. They should see him as a metaphor for the need to be flexible.

In Alex Ross's epic *Earth X* series, which takes place in a dystopian future of the Marvel universe, it is finally explained that, although Richards was brilliant before the accident that made his body ultraflexible, he now uses his newfound malleability to stretch his brain to accommodate and solve almost any problem. This moves Reed to the top of Marvel's list of "Big Brains," alongside Victor Von Doom (aka Dr. Doom) and Henry Pym (aka Yellowjacket).

LESSON 1 What Can You Learn from Mr. Fantastic?

Lesson: Stay Flexible

Just as Mr. Fantastic is able to stretch his brain to solve almost any problem, Business Superheroes need to maintain flexibility in all their problem-solving attempts.

My favorite quote concerning flexibility comes from Talal Abu-Ghazaleh, who is often dubbed the godfather of Arab accounting because his organization employs more than a thousand professionals throughout its fifty-two offices in the Middle East. Abu-Ghazaleh states: "We can never be certain about the future and therefore we must continue to be flexible and adaptable so that we can react quickly to the needs of our clients and our market place."

All those wishing to don the cape and cowl of a Business Superhero need to recognize that Abu-Ghazaleh's words show a truism in business as in life: The future has yet to be written. As such, one needs to continually explore alternative solutions and adapt to an ever-changing landscape at the office and in the field. For when we abandon examining all possible solutions, we run the risk of getting stuck in binary situations with no possible win–win outcome. (For more on ultimatums, see Chapter 11.)

FANTASTIC FOUR: IT TAKES ALL TYPES

The Thing, the Invisible Woman, the Human Torch, and Mr. Fantastic make up the Fantastic Four. Although Mr. Fantastic (profiled in Chapter 24) may get the nod as leader of Marvel's first family, there is more to this team than just Reed Richards.

WHO ARE THE FANTASTIC FOUR?

In the last chapter you met Reed Richards, husband to Sue Storm (the Invisible Woman), brother-in-law to Johnny Storm (the Human Torch), and former college roommate of Benjamin Grimm (the Thing). And you learned how the four of them were exposed to cosmic energy, which gave them powers. But did you know that:

- Sue's the strongest? A Marvel series from the Modern Age depicts Sue Storm and Reed Richards as teenage prodigies, and although Storm isn't the genius her partner is, she is no pushover. In fact, Storm (with her ability to control invisible force fields) is considered one of the Marvel universe's most powerful heroes. While Reed is considered the brains behind the Fantastic Four, it is Storm who is considered the team's soul.

- Thing is a world champion? During a sabbatical from the Fantastic Four, the Thing joined the Marvel universe's own Unlimited Class Wrestling Federation, which pits superpowered contestants against each other inside the squared circle. He spent time as an undefeated champion.
- There has been more than one Human Torch? Johnny Storm is the second Marvel character to use the moniker "Human Torch." Twenty years before the debut of the Fantastic Four, Timely Comics (Marvel Comics' earliest incarnation) featured the Golden Age super-team the Invaders, which included the first Human Torch—an android who could control fire.

WHY DO THE FANTASTIC FOUR MATTER?

When I worked for Ernst & Young's law firm, it soon became apparent that professionals, especially those at larger firms, could be categorized into one of four categories: Finders, Minders, Grinders, and Binders.

Finders, better known today as *rainmakers*, are those who attract and pursue new work. Minders are those who perform administrative tasks and coordinate the efforts of the other three types; they often are charged with keeping the books, invoicing the clients, and paying the bills. Grinders are those who tackle the actual client work, which leaves Binders as those who bring the members of a firm together by (for example) inviting a small group to lunch or recognizing achievements of the firm's employees.

Entrepreneur's Ray Silverstein looks at sales forces in particular, and classifies their members as either Type F (Finders), Type M (Minders), or Type G (Grinders). Finders are the aggressive salespersons who always seek the next big conquest, while Minders nurture the necessary relationships with customers to ensure customer satisfaction and repeat sales. Grinders, on the other hand, tirelessly endure the necessary tasks of locating new leads and maintaining day-to-day operations (see www.entrepreneur.com).

Setting aside the missing Type B in Silverstein's list, one can see the general taxonomy. Although creator Lee based the members of the Fantastic Four on the traditional four elements of nature—fire, water, earth, and air—the superheroes also effectively provide a catalog of the elements that make up a successful corporation:

- Mr. Fantastic is the Binder of the group. Malleable and possessing leadership qualities, it was his actions that led to the group's initial formation.

- ★ The Invisible Woman is the Minder of the team. She manages the group's internal and external relationships.
- ★ The Thing is the Fantastic Four's resident Grinder. Slow and steady, the ever-loving Thing can always be counted on.
- ★ The Human Torch is the Finder of the group, with his power of flight, his charisma, and his thrill-seeker personality.

LESSON 1 What Can You Learn from the Fantastic Four?

Lesson: Know Your Role

The Fantastic Four maintains their preeminence within the Marvel universe through the combined diverse elements of the team members. This creation of a system—in which the whole is larger than the sum of its parts—is possible only when the characters know and embrace their roles, understanding their distinct spheres of authority and responsibility.

For the Business Superhero, knowing and embracing your role as Finder, Minder, Grinder, or Binder will allow you to focus on the actions that magnify profits for all. At my firm, which is one of North America's leading seed venture capital funds, I know I'm the Finder. Although all three partners actively work on deals, I'm the person who serves as the public face of the team. My former college peer Doug Hewson is our managing partner—our Minder if you will; our senior partner, Michael J. Turillo, is

THE FANTASTIC FOUR OF THE REAL WORLD

Sergey Brin and Larry Page may have founded Google, but it was the addition of CEO Eric Schmidt that led to its becoming one of the most valuable companies in the world.

According to insiders, Brin and Page fought like Johnny Storm and Ben Grimm back in the day, but then through collaboration (and success, no doubt) they fell into sync. That was 1995.

In 1996, with some very interesting technology in their pockets, they attracted angel investor Andy Bechtolsheim. According to urban legend in Silicon Valley, Bechtolsheim was so impressed by the demo, he wrote out a check for $100,000 to Google Inc. on the spot. This of course was a problem, since the founders had yet to incorporate a legal entity.

Fast forward to 2001, when Google was handling more than 100 million search queries a day and, with its AdWords program, was fast approaching profitability. That is when Schmidt joined. Under Schmidt's leadership, Google went public in 2004. In 2007, less than fifteen years after its inception, Google is worth more than $200 billion. Now *that's* fantastic!

the Binder, setting the overall strategy and direction for the team. The three of us are able to focus on future successes because Dennis Ensign, our CFO and Grinder, keeps the day-to-day operations working smoothly.

I knew when I founded the firm that I wanted partners whose skills were not only complementary to mine but contrary as well. I learned this from a fabulous book called *Founders at*

Work—a collection of interviews with the founders of some of the world's most successful technology companies (including Apple, Flickr, Lotus, PayPal, and Hotmail), where they relate some of the lessons that they learned while building their companies. The greatest lesson I learned from this rich tome was to find partners who are masters of what I suck at. The founders of companies such as Microsoft, eBay, Research in Motion, and Google have all followed this approach.

PLASTIC MAN: HAVE FUN

One of the few characters who has stayed consistent since his birth in the Golden Age of Comics, Plastic Man has never managed to achieve mass appeal, despite his status as a favorite of many of the industry's most important modern creators. Included on that list are Justice League writer Grant Morrison, who featured the malleable crime fighter prominently; painter Alex Ross, who used Plastic Man on many a cover (and even a collector's plate); and the legendary Frank Miller, who depicted the character as one of the DC universe's most powerful heroes in his acclaimed series *The Dark Knight Strikes Again*.

WHO IS PLASTIC MAN?

Before Stan Lee and Marvel's House of Ideas illustrated the power of redemption through Doctor Strange and Iron Man, there was Plastic Man. Plastic Man begins as a thief named Patrick "Eel" O'Brian, who reforms after a botched robbery in which his cohorts abandon him at the scene of the crime, after he's been shot and covered in a mysterious vat of unknown chemicals.* Like so many other accidents from the Golden Age of Comics, O'Brian gains powers from the accident and dedicates himself to making up for his past by joining the FBI.

WHY DOES PLASTIC MAN MATTER?

Besides offering a vivid demonstration that people can evolve and make up for their past sins (see also Chapter 23), Plastic Man illustrates the power of fun.

Throughout his career, writers and artists have always gone to great lengths to leverage Plastic Man's malleability, for slapstick sight gags. In fact, he is often used as a foil for more stoic heroes, like the Martian Manhunter and Batman. Notwithstanding his lighthearted nature, Plastic Man is no less of a dedicated crime fighter than the others and has earned the respect of those with whom he serves.

*Mysterious vats of chemicals seem to pervade the comic universe. The original Flash's origin also involved a mysterious vat of chemicals, as do the origins of the Joker, the Creeper, and Spider-Man's foe Tombstone.

LESSON 1 What Can You Learn from Plastic Man?
Lesson: Have Fun at Work

Lawrence Lewin is a Business Superhero, many times over. The UK-born Lewin cofounded lingerie retailer La Senza in 1990, selling it fifteen years later to the parent company of Victoria's Secret for over $700 million. Not bad for a guy who is into women's underwear. I had the chance to interview Lewin when he was a panelist on the CBC's venture capital business reality show *Dragons' Den*. During the interview, I asked him his best business lesson, to which he answered: "Whatever you do, enjoy it; have a good time."

Have fun? Seems somewhat strange coming from a multimillionaire, but not when we discussed it further. By talking with the silver-haired czar of underwear, I learned about Lewin's philosophy: To dedicate yourself fully to a task, you not only have to be passionate about it (see Chapter 20) but you have to enjoy doing it because success comes only from hard work, and hard work seems easier when you're having fun. Further, being a Business Superhero is plenty time-consuming, and since you're going to be spending so much time on business matters, you should make sure you enjoy that time.

Lewin isn't alone in his belief. Wal-Mart Founder Sam Walton also espoused the virtues of taking an easygoing approach to business when you can. Walton promoted his lighthearted approach religiously: "Don't take yourself so seriously. Loosen up, and everybody around you will loosen up. Have fun." He explained, "My feeling is that just because we work so hard, we don't have to go around with long faces all the time. While we're doing all of this work, we like to have a good time."

I can't stress this point enough. As discussed earlier, Business Superheroes must dedicate themselves to being the best (see Chapter 15). But doing so requires a considerable amount of time and effort. To facilitate that commitment, Business Superheroes should ensure that they are not only passionate about what they are pursuing but can have fun doing it. Otherwise, the personal cost will grow exponentially. To illustrate this, consider your perception of time: When you are doing something that is boring, time seems to slow down, and everything seems to drag out. Yet when you are engaged in a fun activity, time seems to elapse much more quickly. Because you are going to work 40+ hours a week, do you want that time to seem like 100 hours or 10 hours? So make the effort to inject some fun into your work. In fact, follow this formula: The more boring or dull the task, the more fun needs to be injected.

When I was a young lawyer, one of my duties was to put together transactional closing books. Those books contained thousands of pages of fine print and hundreds of legal documents. The task would often take three or four people six or seven hours to complete. It was monotonous, to say the least. Knowing that, I added some fun into the process by getting my peers to see the task as a game—one in which we could compete against each other and against ourselves. Now, this didn't make the work take less time, but it sure made it seem that way.

THE LEGION OF SUPER-HEROES: THE POWER OF DIVERSITY

"Long live the legion" is a battle cry that has inspired comic book teens to action for over thirty years. The three founding members of the Legion of Super-Heroes first appeared in DC Comics' *Adventure Comics* #247 (1958), as a supporting cast for the adventures of Superboy. Despite that secondary status, they hold the title of the comic universe's first team of teenaged superheroes, having been introduced five years before DC's Teen Titans and Marvel's X-Men.

The Legion's popularity eventually eclipsed Superboy's own, as is indicated by the evolution of comic book titles. In the 1970s, *Superboy Starring the Legion of Super-Heroes* became *Superboy and the Legion of Super-Heroes*; the 1980s saw Superboy further relegated to serving as a simple character in the cast of the newly titled *Legion of Super-Heroes*.

WHAT IS THE LEGION OF SUPER-HEROES?

Thousands of years in the future, the Legion of Super-Heroes was formed. Hailing from more than twenty planets throughout the known universe, the Legionnaires were uniquely superpowered. Consistent with the more sophisticated character-driven plots of the Silver Age of Comics, though, the heroes' conflicts with supervillains may have struck less of a chord with their readers than did their struggles with the complexities of adolescence.

In subsequent years, readers became familiar with the extensive membership and complex history of this thirtieth-century group. The ranks of the Legionnaires swelled to more than thirty heroes from around the cosmos, hailing from different galaxies and even different millennia. The only aspect of this group that might lack imagination and diversity would be the nomenclature of the characters: The founding members Cosmic Boy, Lightning Boy, and Saturn Girl were joined by later additions like Matter Eater Lad, Phantom Girl, and Colossal Boy.

WHY DOES THE LEGION MATTER?

Diversity has always been a part of the Legion of Super-Heroes concept. In the 1960s, diversity meant something different from what it means today. Back in the Silver Age of Comics, diversity meant that every character had a different power, a different homeland, or a different way to contribute to the Legion's success.

Today, diversity means so much more. It means that every member of the Legion has a genuinely different way of perceiving things, of reacting to things, and of contributing to a solution. The Legion of Super-Heroes encompasses members from all walks of life, all backgrounds, all colors (Brianiac 5 is green, Chameleon Boy is orange, Tellus is yellow, Shadow Lass is blue), all shapes (for example, Gates, Tellus, and Quislet are all non-bipedal), and all sizes (take a look at Colossal Boy, Micro Lad, Atom Girl, and Shrinking Violet).

But diversity need not be some abstract concept. Thomas Friedman is one of the many authors who have discussed the globalization of our economy and the impact it has had on diversity. No longer are India and China far-off kingdoms; today, with a click of a mouse, people from around the world can gather, share, and collaborate. This has led to increased heterogeneity in the workforce, which in turn has highlighted the value of diversification. Different people have different perspectives, experiences, and approaches, which allow alternative problem-solving techniques to emerge. One of my favorite books of recent times, James Surowiecki's *The Wisdom of Crowds*, identifies heterogeneity in the workforce as one of the keys to successful group decision making. In fact, Surowiecki routinely cites the need for variety within a crowd, to ensure that decisions are shaped by a sufficient range of approaches, thought processes, and private information.

LESSON 1 What Can You Learn from the Legion?

Lesson: Strength through Diversity

The Legion of Super-Heroes illustrates strength through diversity, which is a concept the Business Superhero should adopt. In their seminal 1999 paper "Diversity and Optimality," Economics professors Lu Hong and Scott E. Page conclude that diversity is at the heart of effective group problem solving.

This claim gained additional support from Surowiecki in his 2004 bestseller. In *The Wisdom of Crowds*, he defends the power of collective wisdom and repeatedly illustrates through anecdotal evidence and scientific testing that, for optimal decision making, it is best to rely on a heterogeneous, decentralized group of decision makers. Each member of the group should bring significantly different backgrounds, experiences, and training to the table.

For the Business Superhero, the lesson is simply this: When building your teams, strive to overcome the human tendency to gather like-minded individuals; instead embrace diversity. Diversity of experience, of vision, and of perspective. Not only because it is the right thing to do but because it leads to the best results.

THE LEGION OF SUPER-HEROES OF THE REAL WORLD

AmeriCredit Inc. is a high-risk credit lender out of Fort Worth, Texas; and it always comes to my mind when I think about diversity. Founded in 1992, in less than a decade this company, underpinned on a foundation of diversity, joined the *Fortune* 1000, with more than $15 billion in managed receivables.

Legend has it that, in 2000, AmeriCredit's then-CEO Michael Barrington once marched a hundred members of senior management from the office to a nearby theater that was showing *Remember the Titans*, starring Denzel Washington.

The movie shows the power of diversity as it tells the true story of a racially diverse high school football team from Alexandria, Virginia. In 1971, the team triumphed, backed by mutual respect and cooperation. When asked about this bold move, Barrington is credited with saying "The movie sends a powerful message about how diverse people can come together to accomplish more as a team."

MIDNIGHTER: PLAY THE MOVIE IN ADVANCE

"I've played this fight in my head millions of times. I know all the moves you will make. I've already won, you just don't know it yet." These chilling words attest to the unique and remarkable power of The Authority's Bringer of Darkness, Midnighter.

Created by writer Warren Ellis and artist Bryan Hitch, Midnighter first appeared in *Stormwatch*, volume 2, #4. Some see the character as a parallel to or reinterpretation of DC Comics' Batman. He and his life partner, Apollo, have also been seen as a parallel of the Batman/Superman "World's Finest" partnership, a comparison that was posited in Rob Lendrum's 2004 essay "Queering Super-Manhood: The Gay Superhero in Mainstream Comic Books" and supported in DC Comics' 2007 *Countdown: Arena* series.

However, significant differences between Batman and Midnighter do exist:

- Midnighter has special powers. Batman does not.

* Midnighter is rarely seen out of costume. Batman actively maintains a secret identity.
* Midnighter is openly gay, happily married, and a devoted parent of an adopted child. Batman is a philandering billionaire playboy when not in costume.

WHO IS MIDNIGHTER?

Created by a power-mad government official, Midnighter is a cyborg who was meant to serve American needs. A super-soldier with enhanced strength, endurance, and reaction time, Midnighter's most famous ability is his power to predict how a battle will unfold before it starts. His "fight implants" include a combat computer, which allows him to run through a given combat situation millions of times in his mind, almost instantly covering nearly every possible result before the first punch is even thrown. He uses this information to predict the actions and/or reactions of his foes, countering their moves almost before they even think to make them. According to Midnighter, his powers also work by letting him see the outcome of the battle he wants and, working backward, enabling him to follow the right steps to achieve it.

WHY DOES MIDNIGHTER MATTER?

Before Midnighter, there were many openly gay (and even more closeted) superheroes. In his seminal list of the fates of gay superheroes, Perry Moore (author of *Hero*, a 2007 novel about a gay superhero coming to terms with his sexuality and powers) outs many characters in superherodom, including Northstar, Karma, Obsidian, and the Rawhide Kid. And although characters have been "written gay" since the 1990s, suffice it to say that the jury is still out on the general handling of gays in comic books. That's not, however, the case with Midnighter. "Midnighter is a wonderful, refreshing break from the way gay superheroes have been relegated to back of the bus or victim status in comic books, historically. He is a total bad ass. Probably the most dangerous and definitely the most popular member of The Authority, regardless of his sexuality," Moore told me when I interviewed him on New Year's Day 2008. Moore added, "One of the greatest things about Midnighter is his love for family. I remember in particular one sequence in a story in which Midnighter is facing a group of deadly super-assassins. He stares them down and says, 'Let's get this over with quick so I can get home and make love to my husband.' "

In other words, Midnighter works to live; he doesn't just live to work. His husband and daughter are what truly inspire him. Moore notes that, while characters like Wolverine (another well-known bad ass) and Batman are isolated on a seemingly permanent basis, Midnighter's "ability to embrace love only seems to enhance his performance, enrich his life, and bring new dedication to his missions."

Midnighter and his husband, Apollo, are consistently portrayed as the more stable members of the super-group The

Authority, particularly when it comes to relationships, sex, and fidelity. Further, to my knowledge, they are the only gay couple to be both life partners and crime-fighting partners (not counting the Ambiguously Gay Duo from *Saturday Night Live*). Finally, they are most certainly the first gay couple in comics to adopt a child.

I hope this trend will continue, and comic books will maintain their traditional role of advocating tolerance and providing vehicles for diversified role models.

LESSON 1 What Can You Learn from Midnighter?

Lesson: Fight First in Your Head

When I analyzed Batman (see Chapter 2), I discussed the value of preparation. I introduced the Green Lantern (see Chapter 3) to discuss the power of visualization. In the character of Midnighter, I see a combination of both. Midnighter's main power is his ability to fight his battles first in his head, before commencing them in the real world. And that is the preeminent lesson to take from this ultimate bad ass.

In 2007, I hired Andrea Chilcote and her team at Morningstar Ventures to become my executive coach. An executive coach is one part Yoda, one part shrink, and one part drill sergeant. Chilcote assisted me with many things, but one of her great lessons was: Play the movie in your head first.

Just like Midnighter, Chilcote takes the time to run through key conversations, presentations, and negotiations in her head before she begins them in real life. If this were a superpower, I'd call it Precognitive Visualization. And it is a superpower that every Business Superhero needs to master.

In business, Precognitive Visualization at a macro level is often referred to as "contingency planning"—an exercise in which management contemplates events that, while unlikely, could be devastating (a hurricane, a power outage, and so on). This exercise is undertaken with great seriousness and depth, not because of the probability of the occurrence but because of the severe consequences of a failure to prepare for it. However, what can be done at a macro level can and should be done at a micro level. Here's how.

The next time you have a big meeting, isolate yourself in a quiet place for a few minutes. Then turn your mind to the meeting. First, remind yourself of the outcome you seek and then review the outcome you think the other parties will be seeking. Then play out all the possible scenarios in your head, focusing most of your time on the most probable outcomes. Play through, line by line, who says what, until you have prepared mentally for all high-probability outcomes. Then go into the meeting. You will find that one of the outcomes you have run through in your head will usually occur in reality. Only now, instead of having to react on the spot, you can reap the benefits of having already thought through your response, and—as Midnighter's iconic role model, Batman, has already shown us—preparation is more than half the battle.

THE MIDNIGHTER OF THE REAL WORLD

McDonald's founder Ray Kroc may seem like an unlikely candidate for the title of Midnighter in the real world. Kroc founded McDonald's in 1955, and within a few decades, he was topping the *Time* 100 list of most influential titans of industry.

Kroc's secret? Visualization. As a student, Kroc rarely devoted himself diligently to his classes, choosing instead to spend most of his time daydreaming about his ambitions, particularly about how he would confront the obstacles that he would face on his road to success. Those daydreams were no idle fantasies—they became vital road maps to success. In *Grinding It Out: The Making of McDonald's*, Kroc wrote: "I have never considered my dreams wasted energy; they were invariably linked to some form of action."

PART III

BRING ON THE BAD GUYS

In the last part of the book I analyzed the lessons that iconic figures like Captain America, Spider-Man, and Green Arrow can teach Business Superheroes about leadership, responsibility, and focus. But what's a superhero without a nemesis? In fact, it is often the villain who completes the hero's mythos. Consequently, no book on superheroes (even the business variety) would be complete without examining the characters we love to hate—the bad guys. For just as superheroes can illustrate best practices for future business superstars, supervillains can alert young Business Superheroes to many of the pitfalls and dangers that attend their calling.

DR. DOOM: AVOID ENLIGHTENED DESPOTISM

One of the few supervillains with diplomatic immunity, Victor Von Doom has plagued the Fantastic Four with his quest for world domination since he first appeared in *Fantastic Four* #5.

WHO IS DR. DOOM?

A brilliant scientist, most accounts of his origin claim that Doom was a college peer of Reed Richards (see Chapter 24) and often competed with him to see whose brilliance shone brightest. Doom became grossly embittered when an experiment went wrong, scarring his face horribly. Blaming Richards for the accident, Doom returned to his home country of Latveria, crowned himself king, and created a high-tech suit of armor, both to cover his deformity and to imbue him with various superpowers, including enhanced endurance and energy blasts.

Doom is one of Stan Lee's most prized creations. Just as Lee added depth to the psyche of his Silver Age heroes, he also imbued his villains with extra psychological complexity and envisioned Doom as an honorable enlightened despot. Over the years, Dr. Doom has been consistently depicted as someone who keeps his word and acts according to his belief in social welfare, even in his pursuit of world domination.

WHY DOES DR. DOOM MATTER?

Enlightened despotism, also known as "benevolent dictatorship," is a political philosophy that casts the leader as the ultimate servant of the state, ruling over his or her people for their own good rather than for tyrannical personal gain. As a practitioner of enlightened despotism, Doom doesn't seek world domination for his own selfish reasons. Rather, he sincerely believes that the world would be a better place under his rule; an argument he has supported by ridding his home country of many of the ills that he blames on Western civilization. As for his continual defeat at the hands of Fantastic Four, Doom concludes that the heroes wish to impose liberty on the population, thus denying the people the universal protection that he believes could be granted under his autocratic rule.

Doom, however, is not alone in his approach. Many a business leader has been called a benevolent dictator, and even more business leaders have been perceived as having King Syndrome.

LESSON 1 What Can You Learn from Dr. Doom?

Lesson: Avoid King Syndrome

I use the term *King Syndrome* to describe enlightened despotism in commerce. Suffering from it is the downfall of many a potential Business Superhero. Business colleagues who suffer from this syndrome may demonstrate any of the following symptoms:

- ★ Use us-vs.-them language
- ★ Are willing to sacrifice team objectives for personal gain
- ★ Abuse power by acting in a petty manner toward juniors
- ★ Reject the ideas of others, believing their own ideas are always best
- ★ Rationalize away injustices done by them or in their name
- ★ Control the flow of information to manipulate others
- ★ Hoard resources and foster the building of silos within an organization

Although most of the symptoms tend to affect the organization at a team level, the last one—building of silos—is more focused on damaging the organization itself. It is a classic tactic undertaken by prospective Dr. Dooms who aim to carve out a fiefdom within their workplaces over which they have sole control (including control of the flow of information), for the purpose of manipulating subordinates, supervisors, or both.

Dr. Carol Kinsey Goman, who helps teams change strategies to address issues such as siloing, includes on her website a telling article titled "The 'Unsiloing' of Organizations." There, she lays out the main forces behind the rise of siloing and the effects of that corporate trend, citing an American Management Association survey that claims 97 percent of executives believe siloing leads to negative outcomes. Its effects can include a loss of overall productivity, a decrease in synergy across teams, and—most important—damage to staff morale. She writes:

> I've seen firsthand what silos can do to an enterprise: The organization disintegrates into a group of isolated camps, with little incentive to collaborate, share information, or team up to pursue critical outcomes.

What started as a morale issue ends up striking at the very heart of a company's productivity, as potential Dr. Dooms divert a company's resources away from its central mission, and direct them instead to personal agendas. The consequent inefficiency reduces the company's employees to internal conflict and feelings of frustration. Happily, Goman also outlines several approaches to tearing down silos, including the following:

- ★ Rewarding collaboration
- ★ Communicating transparently
- ★ Fostering social networks at work
- ★ Aligning all leaders' interests
- ★ Focusing on the customer

By implementing some of these tactics, a business leader will not only help tear down silos at work but will improve the organization's effectiveness, productivity, and unity of purpose. By privileging alignment, transparency, and collaboration, Business Superheroes are likely to avoid becoming (or even being perceived as) enlightened despots like Dr. Doom.

SINESTRO: CHOOSE INSPIRATION OVER FEAR

In blackest day, in brightest night, beware your fears made into light. Let those who try to stop what's right burn like my power . . . Sinestro's might!" These were the words uttered by the Green Lantern's nemesis, Sinestro, to kick off what would be the cosmic comic battle of 2007: *The Sinestro Corps War*.

WHO IS SINESTRO?

Before Hal Jordan became the greatest of the Green Lantern Corps (see Chapter 3) that title was held by Sinestro, who received much initial praise for his unswerving dedication to keeping order in his space sector. However, Sinestro's dedication soon became an obsession, when the pink-skinned native of the planet Korugar confused order with protection. Tyrannizing the very population that he was charged with protecting, Sinestro

soon shaped his planet and sector into a rigid bastion of order, maintained through fascism and fear.

When Hal Jordan joined the corps, Sinestro was assigned to be his mentor and instructor. However, upon reporting for training, Jordan was horrified to learn of Sinestro's despotic methods and soon brought them to the attention of the leaders of the Green Lantern Corps, a decision that would eventually lead to Sinestro's conviction for crimes against the universe and against the corps. As punishment, Sinestro was stripped of his power ring and imprisoned in the antimatter universe.

Unfortunately for Jordan and the Green Lantern Corps,

Sinestro found allies in that prison who supplied him with a yellow power ring that would enable him to return to the positive matter universe and, later, raise an army of fear-based ringslingers, dubbed the Sinestro Corps.

Sinestro and his corps fight to this day to bring order to the universe by instilling fear.

WHY DOES SINESTRO MATTER?

Sinestro was once seen as the greatest hero the corps had ever produced, but by deciding that the laudable goals of law and order justified any means, Sinestro took the dark path of leadership. He decided to use fear to control others. Fear to create order. Fear to accomplish his goals and objectives.

By their very nature, Business Superheroes often ascend to places of leadership within the companies that employ them. Consequently, Business Superheroes are often obliged to decide which style of leadership they wish to pursue. Some follow the path of the hero, harnessing respect and inspiration to guide their teams; others end up like Sinestro and use fear and other negative tactics in an attempt to control their destinies and their staff.

LESSON 1 What Can You Learn from Sinestro?

Lesson: Avoid the Dark Path

We've all seen them—those managers who bully and scream their way to success. Those who threaten and punish until they get what they want. But those victories are often short lived and are never the path of the Business Superhero.

Leadership requires power. That truism applies equally in comics and real life. Just as true is the distinction between positional power and personal power. Positional power is derived from the title you hold, the budget you control, and the authority granted to you by a higher power (like your boss). In her article "Power, Leadership and You," author Michelle Randall's summary of positional power calls to mind the evolution of Sinestro's character:

> By its very nature, positional power is transient. If we become overly seduced by its trappings, we will compromise ourselves and do anything in order to hold on to it. Also, if we lose sight that the power is in the position, not us, we can believe in our own invincibility and start to do things that are just, well, stupid.

Personal power is just the opposite. It originates from internal sources and comes from the relationships you cultivate. Consequently, it permits you to draw on the resources and support of a broad network of people, many of whom you may have absolutely no positional power over whatsoever. Personal power is usually responsible for your positional power in the first place, and it remains long after any positional power you had fades. It is personal power, of course, that Business Superheroes should cultivate.

Further, in the modern age of the free agents and Brand You (see Golden Rule 4: Craft an identity), positional power is becoming less effective than personal power. With the nearly frictionless communication that the Internet now affords us, ideas can travel at unprecedented speeds and in infinite directions. New communication technologies—and the new information networks that they have fostered—have permitted the rise of thought leaders. These people lack centralized positional power, often due to free agency; their power comes solely from others' respect for their expertise. And these thought leaders, with their personal power, are increasingly replacing leaders whose authority is rooted in positional, institutional power.

How to Develop Personal Power

In her article, Randall presents the means for cultivating personal power and for managing positional power:

- **The company you keep.** Sinestro has belonged to the Legion of Doom, the Secret Society, and the Injustice League. Through these choices, he has surrounded himself with other like-minded villains, ensuring there is no one to challenge his misuse of power. The same can happen to Business Superheroes who don't build a network of high-quality peers—peers willing to offer honest and critical feedback when needed and willing to challenge misuse of power. If all your peers are sycophants and villains, your decision making will lack the benefit of a diversity of opinions (see Chapter 27). The only perspectives you will hear will be either your own (reflected back to you) or those shaped by those with ulterior motives.

★ **Authenticity.** Understand who you are and that your character does not depend on the position you hold. Positional power can often tempt you into believing that you are invincible. You must resist that (incorrect) notion at all times, if only because it will prevent you from recognizing the need to prepare adequately (see Chapters 2 and 6).

★ **Vision.** Reaffirm your oath routinely to ensure you consistently adhere to your foremost values (Golden Rule 2: Swear an oath). Positional power can often tempt you to make short-term sacrifices for perceived long-term gains. After all, it is easier to order someone to do something (through positional power) than to inspire him or her to do it (using personal power). Your oath will help you pursue your goals in a manner that's consistent with your values.

- ★ **Simplicity.** The more successful and powerful you become, the easier it is to get caught up in the trappings of power. But Business Superheroes—including the Oracle of Omaha, Warren Buffet—know that by staying true to themselves and keeping their life free of superficial trappings, they run much less risk of being seduced and/or deluded by the power they wield.
- ★ **Humility.** The biblical book of Proverbs tells us "Pride goeth before destruction." Pride, especially the variety in which you think yourself better than others, is the first step to becoming a Business Supervillain. But if you stay humble, attribute your successes to your team (see Chapter 19), and recognize your personal failures (see Chapter 17), then you will increase your personal power and rely less on your positional power. When you set yourself up as unerring and perfect, you have to live up to those impossible standards. And all the while others will be patiently waiting for the inevitable delight of seeing you proven wrong.
- ★ **Self-reflection.** Every once in a while, step back and evaluate yourself (Golden Rule 6: Establish a hideout). Doing so regularly should ensure your vigilance against the encroachment of pride and other undermining flaws.

Power corrupts, and absolute power corrupts absolutely. We can see this at virtually any stage of our lives. Think back to high school gym class or summer camp athletics. Usually two captains were picked, and those captains would then take turns picking their team members. I was often amazed that even this minuscule amount of power could have a negative effect on the team captains, frequently eliciting such qualities as insensitivity, arrogance, and spite. For a workplace example, did you ever have a peer who was promoted to become your boss? Although many people are able to make the transition effectively, my expertise suggests that the majority end up having difficulty remaining humble and managing effective relationships with former peers as they become a boss. Still not convinced? Then turn to the local business media. It is unfortunate (but true) that almost every other week, reports emerge of some heinous abuse of power by the senior management of one company or another. Somewhere along the line, these once-good managers became corrupt dictators of their own fiefdom, betraying the trust placed in them by their companies' owners (the shareholders) and of society at large. By losing sight of ethical values, they compromise their value to their companies and diminish their companies' overall value. Sometimes these executives can become genuine Business Supervillains and, like their comic-book counterparts, a period of incarceration may (but often doesn't) lead them to reform.

MAGNETO: AVOID ZEALOTRY

"Better to live on our feet than to die on our knees!" is a quote often attributed to the Master of Magnetism, the X-Men's number one foe, Magneto. (The original quote actually comes from Emiliano Zapata, Mexican reformer and revolutionary.)

WHO IS MAGNETO?

Created in 1961 by Stan Lee and Jack Kirby, Magneto has been the primary antagonist of the X-Men since he first appeared on the cover of *X-Men* #1. Magneto's fictional biography is as tragic as they come. Born in Germany in the early 1940s he, like most Jews of that time, is persecuted by the Nazis and finds himself sent to Auschwitz. Although Magneto manages to survive Auschwitz, he is forced to bear witness to his family's brutal death at the hands of the Nazis. Many years later, Magneto again becomes a victim of others' prejudice, when the harassment of townspeople and local authorities prevent him from rescuing his daughter in a fire. These early traumas shape Magneto's belief that humans and mutants (those born with powers, like his own control over magnetic forces) will never be able to live in harmony. He subsequently appoints himself protector of mutantkind, with the sole duty of ensuring that mutants don't suffer fates similar to those of his family members.

WHY DOES MAGNETO MATTER?

If Professor Charles Xavier (the leader of the X-Men) is often seen as representing Martin Luther King Jr.'s vision of peaceful assimilation, Magneto represents Malcolm X's belief in a minority's right to defend itself from aggression through the use of force. Both Professor Xavier and Magneto seek a way for mutants to live in peace without fear of persecution, just as both King and Malcolm X shared that goal for African Americans in the 1960s. Because Magneto is often portrayed as an antihero who engages in acts of terrorism against humankind in defense of civil liberties, he serves to illustrate the dangers of being a zealot.

For the aspiring or practicing Business Superhero, Magneto demonstrates the error of placing the ends above the means and of deciding that might makes right. It is interesting to note—particularly given Magneto's personal history—that the term *zealot* dates back to the first century CE, as the name of a sect of fanatical Jews who rebelled against the Roman Empire in Judea;

some Zealots advocated the use of violence in the preservation of their own culture and liberties. In modern times, the term *zealot* is most often used to describe a fervent and even militant proponent of some ideal or cause. Both definitions have meaning for Magneto and for the Business Superhero.

LESSON 1 What Can You Learn from Magneto?

Lesson: Manage your Zeal

As I've discussed extensively, Business Superheroes need to be passionate in the pursuit of their goals. However, Magneto shows that there is a fine line between the passionate pursuit of something and zealotry. As a Business Superhero, you must be particularly sensitive to that difference.

Although it is important for Business Superheroes to pursue their ambitions and those of their immediate teams, they must be aware of how those goals dovetail with the larger organization they serve. David Hurst, in an article titled "Monomaniacs with a Mission," discusses the topic of zealotry as a necessary force of innovation, stating: "[T]he history of innovation in all kinds of organizations, from nations to businesses, is replete with stories of individuals and small groups of people who, through extreme focus, resolve, and passion, have had an impact out of all proportion to their numbers."

Hurst turns to Gary Hamel, author of *Leading the Revolution*, for an example of someone who is "optimistic about the ability of zealots to thrive" within the culture of large corporations. This defense of zealotry is, however, balanced by Hurst with a note of skepticism about whether zealots can "change established organizations"; he introduces Charles Handy's book *The New Alchemists: How Visionary People Make Something Out of Nothing* as an example of a more pessimistic analysis of the ability of zealots to remake established structures and companies through the sheer force of their inspiration and drive.

So how do Business Superheroes ensure they follow Professor Xavier's example and not get caught up in the zealotry of Magneto? I suggest a three-pronged approach:

★ Understand your goals and how they fit into the larger goals of your community (even if that community is a *Fortune* 500 multinational corporation).
★ Test your approach against the standard of your oath (Golden Rule 2: Swear an oath).
★ Understand that sometimes short-term battles need to be lost for ultimate victory to be won.

LEX LUTHOR: EGO CHECK

He ranked fourth in the 2005 *Forbes* Fictional 15 list of richest characters. *Wizard: The Guide to Comics* magazine ranked him as the eighth-greatest villain of all time. He has also been hailed as the Smartest Person on Earth in the DC universe, beating out both Ray Palmer (aka the Atom) and Bruce Wayne (aka Batman). He is the bald-headed billionaire Lex Luthor.

WHO IS LEX LUTHOR?

Although he debuted in 1940 in *Action Comics* #23, Luthor's conception seems to predate Superman's own. In 1933, Superman's eventual creators (Jerry Siegel and Joe Shuster) wrote a short story titled "Reign of the Superman," but the Superman of that story was not an alien superhero protecting truth and justice—he was, like Luthor, a bald-headed villain bent on world conquest.

Over the years, Luthor has been reimagined to keep up with

the times. In the 1940s he was a mad scientist, in the 1980s a corporate raider. Most recently, he has been president of the United States. It is interesting to note that, if Superman is a metaphor for all we want to be, Luthor may embody our society's most pressing fears (for example, nuclear war in the forties, corporate greed in the eighties, political corruption in the new millennium).

Notwithstanding his many incarnations, two things have always stayed consistent in the Luthor mythology: (1) his belief that he is entitled to rule the world and (2) his hatred of Superman, who represents the only true threat to his plans for world dominance. The nature of Luthor's hatred for the Last Son of Krypton has, however, evolved over time.

In recent years, Luthor's rhetoric emphasizes Superman's alien status, arguing that he cannot be trusted and is a threat to the security of humankind. But the pathological nature of that hatred indicates a deeper psychological issue. In the 1980s, Luthor's hatred was rooted in simple jealousy: Before Superman's arrival, Luthor had been the most powerful and loved man in Metropolis—fame that was stolen "faster than a speeding bullet" when Superman came on the scene.

Luthor's recent denunciations of Superman have adopted the discourse of racial supremacy and eugenics, with Luthor charging that Superman is hindering the human race's own evolutionary development. Lex's own misguided interpretation of Darwin's theory of natural selection believes that the notion of evolutionary progress through "survival of the fittest" necessarily requires the elimination of the weakest elements in society. For this reason, he sees the Man of Steel as obstructing the process of natural selection by protecting humankind from the challenges that are at the heart of evolution (and their consequences). He similarly claims that society's reliance on Superman limits spiritual evolution by preventing humanity from attaining its own superiority and self-sufficiency. Regardless of his motives, Luthor continues to be one of the biggest threats in Superman lore.

WHY DOES LEX LUTHOR MATTER?

In his highly recommended book *Our Gods Wear Spandex*, Christopher Knowles links the creation of Luthor with the rise of UK occultist and controversial figure Aleister Crowley. Crowley and Luthor are similar in both beliefs and appearances. They also both share a penchant for forming secret societies: Crowley was active in occult organizations including the Golden Dawn and Ordo Templi Orientis, while Luthor belonged to the Injustice League and the Legion of Doom, among others.

While some might cite Luthor's unwavering focus on success as the lesson that Business Superheroes can take from the archvillain, I prefer to focus on Lex's Achilles' heel: his ego.

LESSON 1 What Can You Learn from Lex Luthor?

Lesson: Keep Your Ego in Check

What role does ego play in the lives of Business Superheroes? Quite a bit, actually. In a 2005 *Business Week* interview, award-winning researcher Brian Wu contradicts the conventional wisdom that successful entrepreneurs embrace risk more than the average person. Instead, Wu argues that they welcome risk no more than the rest of us, but that confidence in their own abilities leads entrepreneurs to underestimate risks to the point where they may fail to recognize the possibility of negative outcomes. According to Wu:

> Entrepreneurs, like everybody else, hate uncontrollable risks, but on the other hand, they're overconfident in their own abilities—they think they can control their abilities in a random drawing of people. It's like the Lake Wobegon effect in assessing their position among peers. They think they're above the average.

Wu invokes the Lake Wobegon Effect* to describe the natural human tendency to overestimate one's own abilities over the abilities of others. I see this all the time in the venture capital business. In the ten years that I have been in the business of financing startups, I must have heard over 10,000 pitches for investment. Not once has someone pitched me a business that wasn't the next great thing and run by the best founders alive. Heck, I even see this with the venture capital funds themselves, which *all* claim to be top-quartile funds. Once I even heard a great story from a public speaker friend of mine who claimed that, during a graduation address to a medical school, a member of the audience took issue with the speaker's claim that half of the graduating class was below average. Most people simply are unwilling or unable to believe in their own limitations. Just like Lex Luthor.

Now, I'm not suggesting that Business Superheroes don't need self-confidence. In fact, Wu's research proves quite the opposite: Without self-confidence, entrepreneurs would never pursue business dominance, being instead hobbled by a sense of uncertainty and risk. So what's the lesson here for Business Superheroes? Don't believe your own hype—plain and simple.

Warren Buffet, the world's third-richest man, is said to be extremely humble and without ego. He is the anti-narcissist, preferring to avoid the spotlight or a lavish lifestyle—so much so

*This effect is named for the fictional town described on Garrison Keillor's radio show *A Prairie Home Companion*, where "all the women are strong, all the men are good-looking, and"—even more impossible—"all the children are above average."

that he has become no less famous for his humility than for his success. So ask yourself: What do you want to be famous for?

I encourage Business Superheroes to heed Buffet's example and be generous in praise but humble in your self-congratulation and self-promotion. Be economical in your words, thoughtful in your actions, and don't fall into Lex Luthor's trap of letting ego rule. Two ways to jump-start this process are to remember the value of silence (see Chapter 14) and to monitor the portion of your normal daily speech that is devoted to your importance, your abilities, and/or your achievements. By becoming conscious of how much of our thoughts and communications are centered around our ego, we realize just how much that ego actually impedes our ability to achieve our mission. The Business Superhero who is ruled by ego is distracted from his or her focus and has a distorted sense of priorities.

THE JOKER: TOO FAR OUT OF THE BOX

With his bleached white skin and ear-to-ear grin, the Joker has been an evocative image of villainy since he first appeared in *Batman* #1. This nemesis has haunted the Dark Knight for over sixty years, masterminding several of Batman's greatest failures, including the death of Jason Todd (the second Robin) and the crippling of Barbara Gordon (see Chapter 22).

WHO IS THE JOKER?

The Joker arrived on the scene with his acid-squirting lapel flower in the 1940s, but his origins continue to be subject to intense and varied speculation.

One story depicts his earlier years as a small-time hood named Napier. Another version sees him as a failing comic who turns to crime to make ends meet. Another posits that he had a previous arch-villain persona, as Red Hood. Regardless of the character's early history, the Joker's identity is born when he falls in a vat of acid, which grants him his clownlike appearance and robs him of his sanity.

WHY DOES THE JOKER MATTER?

The Joker teaches Business Superheroes the danger of going too far out of the box. For decades, leaders have claimed appreciation for out-of-the-box thinkers. Those who showed innovation, initiative, and freedom from established thinking were said to be in high demand. But as the Joker illustrates, one person's out-of-the-box thinking can be just plain crazy from another person's perspective.

LESSON 1 What Can You Learn from the Joker?

Lesson: Too Far out of the Box Is Just Crazy

The term *out of the box* has entered everyday speech to describe an unconventional way of thinking, or the innovative thoughts that it can provide. Out-of-the-box thinking is free of the limitations that are imposed by custom or expectation. Thia James and Janet Kuhnert attribute the phrase's origin to the influence of the British mathematician Henry Ernest Dudeney, who invented a famous puzzle that challenges the solver to connect nine dots (arranged in a three-by-three square "box" shape) using only four straight lines, without taking one's pencil off the paper. The puzzle can only be solved if at least two of the lines extend "outside the box" of dots. Applied generally, out-of-the-box thinking has come to describe thought that is unencumbered by habit, convention, or unnecessary limitations.

Such thinking is often a boon to business, in that it has the potential to generate new solutions to old problems—solutions that may lead to higher efficiencies and greater profits. Google's give-it-away-for-free business model is based on providing a service (like web searches) to users for free to generate ad revenue far in excess of what could be earned by charging users for that service. This is a prime example of how out-of-the-box thinking can be massively revolutionary and profitable. The entire software as a service industry (in which users log onto a website to use a program such as Google Docs instead of using one that runs off their desktop such as Microsoft Word) has arisen as a result of the changes in commerce that Google's business model has wrought.

Author Michael Lewis has studied out-of-the-box leaders as diverse as Netscape founder Jim Clark and Oakland A's general manager Billy Beane. Specifically, Lewis examined how such businesspeople implemented innovative approaches to problem solving. In a 2006 interview with *Fortune* editor Brian O'Keefe, Lewis states unequivocally: "Where I have encountered greatness, there is an ability to go a different direction from everyone else while behaving with confidence and assurance as if you're just doing it the way things should be done."

From Lewis's interview and writings we can conclude that, for huge wins, you need out-of-the-box thinking or, as Lewis calls it, "the ability to go a different direction." But can you be *too* out of the box? And if so, how can you tell when that's occurring? Like most things in life (and business), it is a matter of degree and perspective.

The most obvious predictable danger is that an out-of-the-box thinker will be labeled as a nonconformist and may receive criticism for not being a team player. Another danger is that, although conforming to best practices will rarely get you in trouble, trying an untried solution may inspire resistance from those who are more comfortable with traditional ways. Worse yet, it may threaten the career of the innovator, if the proposed plan of action doesn't succeed.

So where does the solution lie? As with so many solutions, it depends on each of us individually. I encourage Business Superheroes to constantly challenge themselves to find innovative approaches. However, I also recommend that they do so only after putting great thought into the process, including gaining a clear understanding of why the current solution is in place. While investing time and energy into exploring creative solutions will make you a Business Superhero, doing so blindly will most likely just make you look like a joker.

MYSTIQUE: BE YOURSELF

Most people were first introduced to the character of Mystique in the 2000 film *X-Men*. Mystique is the naked, blue-skinned henchman of the arch-villain Magneto, and while Rebecca Romijn's on-screen portrayal increased the character's visibility, Mystique predates the film by more than thirty years.

WHO IS MYSTIQUE?

In 1978, Dave Cockrum created a potential arch-nemesis for Ms. Marvel (no relation to Captain Marvel, discussed in Chapter 8). Longtime X-Men scribe Chris Claremont dubbed her Mystique. Mystique, whose natural appearance includes blue skin and yellow eyes, is said to be the ultimate impersonator, with the mutant power to shapeshift into any person who she has ever seen. This

Mystique may have been Rebecca Romijn's first connection to superheroes, but it certainly wasn't her last. She went on to play a role in the 2004 film *The Punisher*. Coincidentally, she is now married to Jerry O'Connell, whose first TV role was as the superhero protagonist of the Canadian television show *My Secret Identity*.

has allowed her to assume a multitude of identities: In her thirty-year career, she has played both sides against the middle, serving Magneto and his Brotherhood of Evil Mutants, before later serving as leader of the X-Factor and even serving as a spy for Charles Xavier's X-Men. If that weren't confusing enough, she is also the mother of the X-Men's blue-skinned teleporter, Nightcrawler, the foster mother of the X-Men's Rogue, and (to balance the ledger between good and evil) has even borne the child of Wolverine's arch-nemesis Sabretooth.

WHY DOES MYSTIQUE MATTER?

A recurring villain in both *Ms. Marvel* and *The X-Men*, Mystique has often facilitated writers in many aspects of plot development. In fact, it is fair to say that when the writers for Marvel need to add a twist to the story line Mystique has consistently been a go-to gal, given her mutant ability to be most things to most people.

LESSON 1 What Can You Learn from Mystique?

Lesson: Don't Be All Things to All People

In today's business world, we're often asked to become like Mystique and be all things to all people. However, while flexibility is a virtue, it carries with it the risk of losing yourself, which can cause you ultimately to become no things to no people. This is particularly true in the world I work in most: startups.

In the world of startups, resources are finite, and founders are constantly forced to take on more tasks than they are equipped to handle. Now, I'll be the first person to encourage this behavior: It promotes personal growth and it can give managers (or future managers) an intimate understanding of all the roles they are tasked to lead. Nevertheless, one has to remember Economics 101, particularly the theory of Comparative Advantage.

Comparative Advantage theory explains why oranges are grown in Florida and hockey players in Canada. In a nutshell, it says that efficiencies can be gained if producers focus their resources and efforts on the tasks for which they have a natural competitive advantage. For instance, my learning disability makes keeping track of numbers hard but speaking on my feet easy. So the theory of Comparative Advantage states that I should focus on public speaking and not accounting.

The same is true for Business Superheroes, who need to be team players and wear many hats but who also must avoid trying to be all things to all people. If they get stuck doing things for which they genuinely don't have an aptitude (things that will, therefore, take them longer to complete), they risk being unable to focus on the tasks for which they have an advantage. The result? Their efforts can end up being so watered down as to be virtually ineffective. End of advantage.

CATWOMAN: PERSPECTIVE MATTERS

Catwoman has been played by some of the most beautiful femmes fatales in film and television: Julie Newmar, Eartha Kitt, Lee Meriwether, Michelle Pfeiffer, and Halle Berry. While each actress brought her own unique flair to the character, all portrayed her as a conflicted antihero who splits her time between committing nonviolent crimes and flirting with Batman.

WHO IS CATWOMAN?

Catwoman has been a mainstay of the DC Comics canon since the spring of 1940, when she first appeared in *Batman* #62. Over the decades, this leather-wearing, whip-carrying, cat-inspired villain has been a staple in Batman's supporting cast. She received her own title in 1993, after the popularity of Michelle Pfeiffer's portrayal in Tim Burton's film *Batman Returns*.

WHY DOES CATWOMAN MATTER?

The sensual and morally ambiguous Catwoman is often used as a foil, in contrast to the rationality and uprightness of more traditional heroes like Batman. Since her first appearance, Catwoman has been (among other things) an amnesiac flight attendant, a prostitute with a heart of gold, and a cat burglar. Throughout her many incarnations, however, one fact has always remained constant: Catwoman plays both sides to her advantage. She has teamed up with supervillains such as the Penguin and Lex Luthor and with superheroes such as Batman and the Birds of Prey (see Chapter 22).

LESSON 1 What Can You Learn from Catwoman?

Lesson: Don't Play Both Sides

Sooner or later, all Business Superheroes are put in awkward positions. Positions that require them to walk the extremely fine line between different parties. For me, this happened a few months into my first managerial role at a large multinational accounting firm.

In that role, I was the intermediary between senior management and my team. My loyalties were first tested when it came to laying off employees. The firm was in a downswing and required cutbacks across the company, including in my team. To make matters worse, senior management required that I not disclose layoff information until the actual day the terminations took place. I was conflicted because good leadership requires some degree of transparency and full disclosure. Worse yet, I knew that one of my staff was contemplating buying a large new home and taking on a mortgage that, if he lost his job, would surely overwhelm his fiscal means.

I was in a quandary and was very tempted to tell each side what it wanted to hear. In the short run, that would have mitigated the tension that comes with layoffs; however, eventually all things come to the light, and if I had played both sides, then either management or my team would feel I couldn't be trusted.

So what did I do? Like Catwoman, I made my own path and refused to be stuck in the untenable position into which I was placed (for more, see Chapter 11). In the end, I informed management that I wanted a chance to place those who were to be laid off instead of having to terminate them. This reduced the negative outcomes of the layoffs and allowed me to champion both management's interest (in cutting costs) and my team's interest (in keeping their jobs). More important, it allowed me to avoid being crushed by the competing demands of two factions, and I avoided playing one side off the other.

LESSON 2 What Can You Learn from Catwoman?
Lesson: Perspective Changes Everything

I've saved one of the most important Business Superhero lessons for the last, and while this lesson applies to most people (including many of our heroes and villains), I believe Catwoman illustrates it best. Our opinion of Catwoman can change—we see her one day as a villain, another day as a hero, another day as a victim. In other words, perspective matters. And that's the lesson I'd like to leave you with.

When I was a first-year lawyer, I worked 70 to 80 hours a week and was required to bill clients at least 2,100 hours annually. I am not unique in this: This intense commitment to work is true of all Wall Street lawyers and is probably equally true of most people in their first years of their career. Of course, like most young professionals fresh from school (and its more relaxed lifestyle of late-night drinking and early-morning sleeping), this schedule was quite overwhelming for me. It got so bad that I sometimes complained about my situation endlessly and sometimes I could even be found wallowing in my own misery.

Then I met Frank Sanitate. Frank was (and is) a guru on time management. He is also the author of *Don't Go to Work Unless It's Fun!* (for more on fun at work, see Chapter 26). My employer had brought Frank in during the dreaded February doldrums. His goal was to help us manage both our work and our personal time better, and Frank taught me something that changed my life.

Frank shared with me his secret, and I'll paraphrase it here: "Change your glasses and you change how you see." By *glasses* I'm referring not to the actual eyewear on your face but to the proverbial rose-colored glasses worn by people who project cheerful optimism in all they do. According to Frank, the glasses you wear (be they rose-colored or muddy) affect your experience of the world and, more specifically, your experiences at work. Changing your perception changes your performance, which changes other people's perception of you. Perspective matters.

Frank showed me that something as simple as changing the language we use to describe our experience can modify that experience. My mother, Bev Wise, taught me this exact lesson in a different form. She preached to me from an early age: "The only thing worse than being too busy? Not being busy at all."

So if you repeat to yourself over and over again that you are overwhelmed, you will feel overwhelmed. If you are thankful to have a job and be busy, then your workload might not lessen, but it will feel more like a worthwhile challenge than like a burden, and that, in turn, will increase your satisfaction with your life inside and outside of your workplace.

"Change your glasses, and you change how you see" has stuck with me since I met Frank and has become one of the greatest lessons that I try to pass on to all Business Superheroes.

CATWOMAN OF THE REAL WORLD

Michael Lee-Chin was born to a single mother in Jamaica in 1951. He is now one of the richest men in the world, with a personal worth set at more than $2 billion.

Lee-Chin is famous for many things. Two of my favorites are these:

★ Growing his mutual fund company's holdings from less than $1 million to over $12 billion in under two decades
★ His positive attitude

I have had the pleasure of being inspired by a personal encounter with Lee-Chin. I attended a celebration of entrepreneurship in his honor, when, as if channeling both my mother and Frank Sanitate, he paraphrased personal success guru Napoleon Hill, saying: "What the mind can conceive and the heart believe, we can achieve."

APPENDICES

THE BUSINESS SUPERHERO MNEMONIC

When thinking about writing this book, I realized I was going to be conveying huge amounts of information: Information about superheroes, information about businesspeople, and, of course, information about Business Superheroes. So I decided that, like Captain Marvel (see Chapter 8), I needed a magic word or mnemonic to assist me in tying all of these concepts together. At the start of the book, I discussed the concept that all Business Superheroes need to be HEROIC: honorable, extraordinary, relentless, outspoken, inspirational, and courageous.

Now, at the conclusion of the book, I'd like to introduce one last mnemonic to help you remember its key lessons. I've named it in honor of the most litigated character in comic history, Captain Marvel. I call it the SHAZAM! mnemonic, and it pretty much summarizes what I consider to be the top lessons conveyed in this book.

S is for silence is golden. Listen twice as much as you speak.

***H* is for hone your skills.** Preparation leads to victory.
***A* is for avoid ultimatums.** Don't buy into binary outcomes; change the rules if you need to.
***Z* is for zero tolerance for fear.** Overcome fear to become a superhero.
***A* is for arrogance is the enemy within.** Pride goeth before destruction.
***M* is for multitask synergistically.** Build once, sell twice, bill three times.

From the leader of the Inhumans, Black Bolt, we learned the value of silence. Remember we have two ears and only one mouth, so we should be listening at least twice as much as we are talking.

From Batman we learned the value of preparation and the need to hone our skills.

The Silver Surfer taught us to avoid ultimatums and instead change the rules, creating new solutions, one of which (we hope) will be win-win.

Everyone is afraid at times, but the Green Lantern showed us that overcoming fear is a necessary trait of all members of the Green Lantern Corps, so establish zero tolerance for allowing fear to hold you back.

Lex Luthor served as a cautionary tale against the pitfalls of arrogance.

Jamie Madrox, the Multiple Man, illustrated the principle of multitasking synergistically, a theory I call the Double Dip.

Put them all together and you get *SHAZAM!*

THE TEN GOLDEN RULES FOR ALL ASPIRING SUPERHEROES

Rule	
1. Do no evil	*Karma's the worst supervillain*
2. Swear an oath	*The purpose-driven hero*
3. Establish your MO	*Work/life balance*
4. Craft an identity	*Building Brand You*
5. Keep your secrets	*Confidentiality at work*
6. Establish a hideout	*Everyone needs a Batcave*
7. Keep odd hours	*Early rise, early wise*
8. Be ready for team-ups	*1 + 1 = more, in the hero business*
9. Patrol often	*Network, network, network*
10. Overcome adversity	*Overcoming obstacles*

BUSINESS SUPERHERO LESSONS LEARNED

Batman: Preparation Leads to Success

- ⋆ Success is 90 percent preparation
- ⋆ Have the right tools
- ⋆ Even loners need support

The Green Lantern: The Will and the Way

- ⋆ Match wits with your fear
- ⋆ Wisdom + willpower = results
- ⋆ Remember to recharge your battery
- ⋆ Everyone has a boss

Deadman: Gain Perspective

- ⋆ Walk in the shoes of another

Spawn: Think Before You Act

- ★ Karma's a bitch
- ★ Be careful what you wish for

Superman: Know Your Weakness

- ★ Know your kryptonite

Robin: Learn from Others

- ★ Find a mentor

Captain Marvel: SWIPE Often

- ★ SWIPE from the best

Thor: Look for Opportunities

- ★ See opportunity where others don't

Hellboy: Create Your Destiny

- ★ You make your own destiny

The Silver Surfer: Outwit Ultimatums

- ★ Don't buy into ultimatums

The Hulk: Keep Your Cool

- ★ Don't get angry

Wonder Woman: Stay Focused

- ★ Have a mission

Black Bolt: Silence Is Golden

- ★ Active listening
- ★ The value of silence

Wolverine: Strive for Excellence

- ★ Be the best at what you do

Iron Man: The Need for Continuous Improvement

- ★ Pursue lifelong learning and continual improvement

Spider-Man: With Great Power Comes Great Responsibility

- ★ Take responsibility

Madrox: Synergistic Multitasking

- ★ Reap the most rewards

Justice League: Even Superheroes Need Help

- ⋆ Life is a team sport
- ⋆ Role players do just that

Green Arrow: Target a Niche

- ⋆ Find your niche

Captain America: Leadership Best Practices

- ⋆ Lead from the front
- ⋆ Be your brand
- ⋆ Rebel against wrong

Oracle: Build a Network

- ⋆ Cultivate sources

Doctor Strange: Never Too Late to Change

- ⋆ Never too late

Mr. Fantastic: Be Flexible

- ⋆ Stay flexible

Fantastic Four: It Takes All Types

- ★ Know your role

Plastic Man: Have Fun

- ★ Have fun at work

The Legion of Super-Heroes: The Power of Diversity

- ★ Strength through diversity

Midnighter: Play the Movie in Advance

- ★ Fight first in your head

Dr. Doom: Avoid Enlightened Despotism

- ★ Avoid King Syndrome

Sinestro: Choose Inspiration over Fear

- ★ Avoid the dark path

Magneto: Avoid Zealotry

- ★ Manage your zeal

Lex Luthor: Ego Check

- ★ Keep your ego in check

Joker: Too Far out of the Box

- ★ Too Far out of the Box Is Just Crazy

Mystique: Be Yourself

- ★ Don't be all things to all people

Catwoman: Perspective Matters

- ★ Don't play both sides
- ★ Perspective changes everything

COMIC BOOKS 101

While a detailed understanding of the history of comic books isn't necessary for an understanding of the ideas in this book, the business of superhero comics nevertheless provides an interesting and relevant context for the book's lessons. The comic book industry has for decades been an amazingly creative one, responding to (and shaping) cultural trends and issues.

THE INDUSTRY PLAYERS

There are thousands of small, independent publishers of comics—including Arcana, which publishes the comic book that I write, *Tales of Penance*. However, four major publishers make up 90 percent of the comic industry.

DC Comics

DC Comics is the home of Batman, Superman, Wonder Woman, the Justice League, the Legion of Super-Heroes, and the Green Lantern (my favorite). Founded in 1934 as National Allied Publications, DC Comics (now owned by Warner Brothers) is one of the largest English-language publishers in the world. Diamond Comic Distributors reports that DC titles account for more than 30 percent of total comic sales.

Marvel Comics

Marvel Comics is the home of Spider-Man, Iron Man, the Fantastic Four, the X-Men, and the Hulk. Marvel Comics (founded as Timely Comics in 1939) is known especially for the works of revolutionary comic visionaries Stan Lee, Jack Kirby, and Frank Miller. Marvel is currently the bestselling publisher of comics; Diamond Comic Distributors reports that Marvel titles account for more than 35 percent of total comic sales.

Image Comics

Image Comics was founded in the early 1990s by a handful of top writers and artists who broke away from Marvel and DC, seeking increased ownership and creative control over their comic creations. The Image universe is home to Spawn, the Savage Dragon, and Witchblade.

Dark Horse Comics

Dark Horse Comics was founded in 1986 and touts itself as the largest independent publisher, with its titles making up more than 5 percent of total comic sales. It is home to the likes of Hellboy, the Mask, and Sin City.

A (HEAVILY ABRIDGED) HISTORY OF COMICS

Comic books can trace their roots to the pulp stories published in the 1930s and 1940s—most notably the Shadow and Doc Savage. The concept of the superhero, of course, draws from Friedrich Nietzsche's work on the Superman (or Übermensch) but also has at its foundations biblical legends like that of Samson and mythical stories like those of Jason and the Argonauts, Hercules, and Achilles. Notwithstanding their rich prehistory, the comic books of today can trace their direct lineage fundamentally to the early 1930s. The almost eighty years thereafter can be broken down into four distinct ages.

The Golden Age of Comics

The Golden Age of Comics lasted from the 1930s into the early 1950s. Superman, Batman, and Wonder Woman were born in this period. This age is typically seen as dominated by one-dimensional, altruistic characters drawn in a simple style. In 1954, psychiatrist Frederic Wertham wrote, *The Seduction of the Innocent*, which condemned comic books as a cause of juvenile delinquency. This inspired something of a U.S. Congressional witch hunt against comics, resulting in the formation of an external agency known as the Comics Code Authority, which was to police the content of comic books. The industry suffered greatly.

The Silver Age of Comics

The Silver Age of Comics ran from the late 1950s through the 1970s. Stan Lee and Jack Kirby revitalized comic books and turned Marvel Comics into the "House of Ideas," creating the likes of Iron Man, Spider-Man, the Hulk, and the X-Men in a few years of unprecedented creative productivity. Comic art became more complicated, as did the story lines. Heroes became more nuanced and often seemed to be plagued with as many personal problems as the supervillains they fought.

The Dark Age of Comics

The decade lasting from the mid-1980s to the mid-1990s was the next distinctive era of comics, and is often referred to as the Modern Age or Dark Age of Comics. *The Watchmen, The Dark Knight Returns,* and Wolverine are all cornerstones of this era, which saw heroes become still more psychologically complex and much darker. Near the end of this age, characters were becoming so ingrained in realism they no longer wore the characteristic bright costumes, instead donning clothing more appropriate to *The Matrix* movie trilogy. This Dark Age also saw the rise of the hero as a killing machine (see Wolverine, the Punisher, and anything Rob Liefeld has ever touched).

In his fabulous book *Our Gods Wear Spandex: The Secret History of Comic Book Heroes,* Christopher Knowles calls this the "Chromium Age" because of the ubiquitous "chromium foil ultra-special-edition" covers put out by publishers, who wanted to convince a new generation of collectors that these would eventually gain extraordinary value and thus readers should purchase multiple copies of the same comic. This era also saw the birth of Image Comics.

I concur with Knowles's supposition that the Dark Age clearly ended in 1996, with Alex Ross and Mark Waid's *Kingdom Come.* This iconic book sees a younger, more violent generation of heroes (who seem highly reminiscent of the work of Rob Leifeld and Todd MacFarlane) bringing humanity to the brink of nuclear holocaust. In the end, only a resurgence of true superherodom (represented by the Silver Age heroes' coming out of retirement) saves the day.*

The Modern Age of Comics

The rejection of the Dark Age of Comics implied in *Kingdom Come* would (along with a rising geek culture) lay the foundation for a recognizably new Modern Age of Comics beginning in 2002. Industry columnist and historian Peter Sanderson has dubbed it the "Neo-Silver Age" because publishers returned to their Silver Age roots, and superheroes returned to wearing costumes. This age has also been seen as an integration of Silver Age values with the art and depth of the Dark Age. The resurgence of comics has also extended to other media, as many talents have crossed over to movies and television, and vice versa.

**Kingdom Come* is definitely in my top-five list. Also on the list are Moore's *Watchmen* and Miller's *Dark Knight*. The remaining two comics on my personal list are Brian Michael Bendis's *Powers: Who Killed Retro Girl?* and *Sin City*, also by Miller.

INDEX

A

Abu-Ghazaleh, Talal, 158
Academy of Achievement, 73
Achilles' heel, 69
Action Comics #1, 66
Action Comics #23, 200
Adams, Neil, 58
ad hoc work groups, 27
Adventure Comics #247, 169
adversity, 34–37
  failures, famous, 36–37
  handling, 34–36
  positive outcomes of, 37
AdWords, 163
A&E Biography, 60
"*Aharai!*" (after me), 146
Al Simmons, 62
Ali, Muhammad, 90
All's Well That Ends Well (Shakespeare), 5
Ambiguously Gay Duo, 177
American Management Association survey, 186
AmeriCredit Inc., 173
anger control, 97–100, 227
Apple, 164
Aquaman, 14, 57, 135, 137, 138
Arcana, 231
Arena: Countdown, 174
Arrow, 140
Art of the Start, The (Kawasaki), 105
authenticity, 193

B

Barbara Gordon, 149, 150
Barrington, Michael, 173
Barry Allan, 68
Batman, 41–46
Batman Returns, 214
Batman: The Dark Knight Returns, 34
BATNA, 59

"Battlin' Jack" Murdock, 34–35
Bat Whispers, The, 41
Beane, Billy, 208
Bechtolsheim, Andy, 163
benevolent dictatorship. *See* enlightened despotism
Berry, Halle, 214
Big Moo, The, 104
Billy Batson, 75–76
binders, 160, 161–162
Birds of Prey, 150
Black Bolt, 106–112
Blank, Arthur, 87, 120
Bloomberg, Michael, 90
Bono, 125
Bowerman, Bill, 49
"Brand Called You, The" (Peters), 17–18
"Brand You," 15–18, 192
Brand You50, The (Peters), 17
Branson, Richard, 55
Brave and the Bold, The, 26
Brave and the Bold #28, The, 134
Brin, Sergey, 163
Brubaker, Ed, 144
Bruce Banner, 68, 97–98
Bruce Wayne, 5, 42, 68, 200
Buddha, 49–50
Buffet, Warren, 194, 204–205
Built from Scratch (Blank and Marcus), 120
Burton, Tim, 214
Business Superhero-in-Training (BSIT), 27
Business Week, 156, 203
Byrne, Olive, 102
Byrne, Rhonda, 49

C

Captain America, 143–148
Captain Marvel, 75–83
Captain Marvel Adventures, 75
Carnegie, Andrew, 136
Carnegie, Dale, 43, 58, 60, 79, 126
Carter, Linda, 101
Catwoman, 214–219
Centaur Publications, 140
change, adapting to, 153–155, 228
Chilcote, Andrea, 177–178
Chu, Chin-Ning, 86–87
City Slickers, 8
Claremont, Chris, 113, 210
Clark, Jim, 208
Clark Kent, 22, 67, 68
clothing (costumes), 18–19
Cockrum, Dave, 210
Collins, Jim, 141, 142
Comic Books and Graphic Novels: What to Buy (Lavin), 75
Comic Code Authority, 234
company you keep, 192–193
Comparative Advantage theory, 212–213
CreatingMinds.org, 36
crisis, finding opportunities in, 85–87
Crowley, Aleister, 202–203
Crystal, Billy, 8

D

Daredevil, 34–35
Dark Age of Comics, 235–236
Dark Horse Comics, 233
Dark Knight Returns, The, 42
Dark Knight Strikes Again, The, 165
David, Peter, 131
da Vinci, Leonardo, 41
DC Comics, 232
Deadman, 57–60
Deadman Perspective, 58–59
De Cive (Hobbes), 151
destiny, creating, 88–91, 226
  after being fired, 90–91
  free will vs. fate, 89–90
Detective Comics #27, 41
Detective Comics #37, 71
Diamond Comic Distributors, 232
Dick Grayson, 68, 71–72
Dip, The (Godin), 114
Di Pasquale, Norman, 100
disclosure. *See* secrets, keeping
Disney, Walt, 36
Ditko, Steve, 123, 153
diversity, 169–173, 229
"Diversity and Optimality" (Hong and Page), 172
Doc Savage, 23
Doctor Strange, 153–155
Donald Blake, 84–85, 86
Don't Go to Work Unless It's Fun! (Sanitate), 217
Double Dip theory, 132
Douglas, Michael, 3
Downey, Robert, Jr., 117
Dragons' Den, 167
Dr. Doom, 183–187
Dudeney, Henry Ernest, 207–208
Dylan, Bob, 54

E

Earth X series, 157
eBay, 164
Edison, Thomas, 36
ego check, 200–205, 230
Einstein, Albert, 36
elevator pitch, 9–13
Ellis, Warren, 174
enlightened despotism, 183–187, 229
Ensign, Dennis, 163
Entrepreneur, 161
En Vogue Computers, 100
Ernst & Young, 46, 63, 95, 137, 160
excellence, striving for, 113–116, 227
  value in, 115–116
  Zipf's law, 114–115

F

Family Jewels, 15
Fantastic Four, 92–95, 159–164
Fantastic Four #5, 183
Fast Company, 17
fears, 50–52
  see also inspiration and fear, choosing between
Ferrigno, Lou, 97

finders, 160, 161–162
flexibility, 156–158, 228
Flickr, 164
focus, 101–104, 227
Forbes, 5, 17
Ford, Henry, 36
Fortress of Solitude, 23
Fortune, 17, 208
Fortune 500, 80
Fortune 1000, 173
Founders at Work, 163–164
Franklin, Benjamin, 24, 79
"free agent Nation," 15
fun, power of, 165–168, 229

G

Gadna, 145–146
Gaiman, Neil, 70, 77, 78
Galactus, 92–95
Gandhi, 79
Gates, Bill, 125
General Electric (GE), 116, 121
Giant Size Fantastic Four #4, 130
goals, 5
Godin, Seth, 104
Golden Age of Comics, 234
Goman, Carol Kinsey, 186–187
Good to Great: Why Some Companies Make the Leap . . . and Others Don't (Collins), 141
Google, 163, 164, 208
  Docs, 208
  give-it-away-for-free business model, 208
Gordon Gekko, 3–4
Goudey, John, 63
greed, 3–5
Green Arrow, 139–142
Green Lantern, 47–56
Green Lantern Corps, 47–48
Greatness Guide, The (Sharma), 24
Gretzky, Wayne, 49
grinders, 160, 161–162
Grinding It Out: The Making of McDonald's (Kroc), 179
Group of 33, The, 104, 105

H

Hal Jordan, 68, 188–189
Hamel, Gary, 198–199
Handy, Charles, 199
Handy Dan Home Centers, 87
Harper's Monthly, 64
Heck, Don, 117
Hedgehog Concept, 141–142
Hellboy, 88–91
Hero (Moore), 176
Hewlett, Bill, 36
Hewson, Doug, 162
hideouts, establishing, 22–23
Hill, Napoleon, 219
Hitch, Bryan, 174
Hobbes, Thomas, 151
Home Depot, 35, 87, 120
Hong, Lu, 172
Hotmail, 164
House of Ideas, 165

"House of Ideas," 234
How to Win Friends and Influence People (Carnegie), 58, 126
Huang, Jen-Hsun, 51
Hulk, 97–100
human resource (HR) managers/personnel, 45
Human Torch, 159, 160, 162
humility, 194
Hurst, David, 198–199

I

Iacocca, Lee, 90
Ibuka, Masaru, 36
identity, crafting, 15–19
  "brand you," 15–18
  clothing (costumes), 18–19
  consistency, 18
  exercise in, 17
Image Comics, 232–233
improvement, continuous, 117–121, 227
  necessity of, 120
  socially relevant issues, 119
Incredible Hulk #180, 113
inspiration and fear, choosing between, 188–195, 229
  dark paths, avoiding, 191–192
  personal power, developing, 192–195
"Inverse Rule of Scarcity," 29
Invisible Woman, 106, 159, 162
Iron Man, 117–121
Israel Defense Forces (IDF), 146

J

Jacobs, William Wymark, 64
James "Logan" Howlett, 114
Johnny Storm, 159, 160
Joker, 206–209
Jordan, Michael, 49, 138
Journey into Mystery #83, 84–85
Justice League, 134–138

K

karma, 6, 63–64
Kawasaki, Guy, 105
Kennedy, John F., 78
Kingdom Come (Ross and Waid), 235–236
King, Larry, 90
King, Martin Luther, Jr., 197
King Syndrome, avoiding, 185–187
Kirby, Jack, 85, 92, 97, 117, 143, 196, 232, 234
Kitt, Eartha, 214
Knowles, Christopher, 202, 235
Krok, Ray, 36, 179
kryptonite, 69–70

L

Lake Wobegon Effect, 204
La Senza, 167
Lavin, Michael, 75
"Law of Attraction," 49–50, 60
Law of Scarcity, 28
lead by example, 146–147

leadership best practices, 143–148, 228
be your brand, 146–147
examples of, 145
principles of, 146
wrong, rebel against, 147–148
Leading the Revolution (Hamel), 198–199
Lee-Chin, Michael, 219
Lee, Stan, 84, 92, 97, 117, 119, 123, 153, 161, 165, 184, 196, 232, 234
Legion of Super-Heroes, 169–173
Legion of Super-Heroes, 169
Lendrum, Rob, 174
Leviathan (Hobbes), 151
Lewin, Lawrence, 167
Lewis, Carl, 49
Lewis, Michael, 208–209
Lex Luthor, 5, 200–205
Lieber, Larry, 117
Liefeld, Rob, 235
Lincoln, Abraham, 79
listening, 106–112, 227
active, 108–109
silence, value of, 110–112
Lombardi, Vince, 34–35, 79
Lotus, 164
Lucas, George, 133

M

MacFarlane, Todd, 235
MacKay, Harvey, 90
Macy, R. H., 36
Madrox, 130–133
MadroX, 131
Madrox Principle, 132–134
Magneto, 196–199
Magnificent Seven, 135
Make It So: Leadership Leasons from Star Trek, The Next Generation, 20
Malcolm X, 197
Man of Bronze, 23
Marcus, Bernie, 87, 90, 120
Marston, Elizabeth Holloway, 102
Marston, William Moulton, 102
Marvel Comics, 232
Marvelman, 77
Marvel Team-Up, 26
Matt Murdock, 34–35, 68
McDonald's, 36, 179
McFarland, Todd, 78
mentors, 73–74
mentorship, 71–74
Meriwether, Lee, 214
Michelle, Randall, 191
Microsoft, 164
Microsoft Word, 208
Midas, King, 64
Midnighter, 174–179
Mignola, Mike, 88, 89
Miller, Frank, 34, 42, 61, 113, 114, 165, 232
minders, 160, 161–162
Miracleman, 77, 78
mission
creating, 103–105
statement, 10

MO (modus operandi), 13–15
network, plan of attack, 31–34
public identity, 14–15
secret identity, 14
modeling (SWIPE), 75–83, 226
choosing a model, 80, 82
self-assessment, 80
setting up your SWIPE, 81–82
SHAZAM mnemonic, 76–77
skills analysis, 83
things you can SWIPE, 79–80
Modern Age of Comics, 236
"Monkey's Paw, The" (Jacobs), 64
Monk Who Sold His Ferrari, The (Sharma), 7
"Monomaniacs with a Mission" (Hurst), 198
Moore, Alan, 61, 77, 150
Moore, Perry, 176
More Fun Comics, 139
Morita, Akio, 36
Morrison, Grant, 165
Mr. Fantastic, 156–158, 161
Ms. magazine, 103
multitasking
being all things to all people, 212–213
Madrox Principle, 132–133
risks of, 210–213, 230
synergistic, 130–133, 227
My Secret Identity, 211
Mystic, 210–213

N

National Allied Publications, 232
National Collegiate Athletic Association (NCAA), 49
National Financing Forum, 33
Natural Law of Business, 29
Netscape, 208
network, 149–152, 228
cultivate sources, 151–152
MO or plan of attack, 31–34
New Alchemists: How Visionary People Make Something Out of Nothing, The (Handy), 199
New Line Cinema, 61
Newmar, Julie, 214
niche, targeting, 139–142, 228
Nietzsche, Friedrich, 233
Nightwing, 68, 73
Nike, 49
Norrin Radd, 92–93, 95
Nvidia, 51

O

oaths, 6–13
business superhero oath, 7–8
crafting, 9
elevator pitch, 9–13
exercise in, 10
Green Lantern's, 7
need for, 8–9
O'Connell, Jerry, 211
O'Keefe, Brian, 208
Oliver Quinn, 139–140

Operation Rebirth, 144, 145
opportunities, 84–87, 226
  in crisis, 85–87
  seeking, 84–87
Oracle, 149–152
Origin of the Silver Surfer, The, 92
Our Gods Wear Spandex (Knowles), 202, 235
out-of-the-box thinkers
  negative, 206–209, 230
  positive, 92–96, 226
outwit ultimatums. *See* out-of-the-box thinkers

P

Packard, Dave, 36
Page, Larry, 163
Page, Scott E., 172
Palance, Jack, 8
Patrick "Eer" O'Brian, 166
PayPal, 164
personal power, developing, 192–195
perspective
  changing powers of, 217–218
  Deadman Perspective, 58–59
  gaining, 57–60, 225
  playing both sides, avoiding, 215–216
  significance of, 214–219, 230
Peter Parker, 68, 123
Peters, Tom, 17–18
Philbin, Regis, 79
Pink, Don, 15
Pfeiffer, Michelle, 214
Plastic Man, 165–168
"Power, Leadership and You" (Randall), 191
"power ring," 47–48
Precognitive Visualization, 178
preparation, 41–46, 174–179, 225, 229
  fight first in your head, 177–178
  support, need for, 45–46
  tools for success, 44–45
Punisher, The, 211

Q

Quantum Leap, 58
"Queering Super-Manhood" (Lendrum), 174

R

rainmakers, 161
Rama Kushna, 57
Randall, Michelle, 191, 192
Redmoon, Ambrose, 50
Reed Richards, 156–157, 159–160, 183
"Reign of the Superman" (Siegel and Shuster), 200
Remember the Titans, 173
Research in Motion, 164
responsibility, 122–129, 227
  for failure, 125–126

to share, 124–125
three Cs, avoiding, 126–129
Responsibility Assumption, 60
"Ringslinger," 48
Robbins, Lionel, 28
Roberts, Wess, 20
Robin, 68, 71–74
Rockport shoes, 104–105
Romijn, Rebecca, 210, 211
Romita, John, Sr., 113
Ross, Alex, 157, 165, 235
Ross, Bill, 20

S

safe havens (hideouts), establishing, 22–23
Sanderson, Peter, 236
Sandman comic book series, 70
Sanitate, Frank, 217–218, 219
Satriani, Joe, 94
Saturday Night Live, 177
schedule (keep odd hours), 24–25
Schmidt, Eric, 163
Schwartz, Julius, 47
Secret, The (Byrne), 49
secrets, keeping, 19–22
office parties, 21–22
one-way communication policy, 21
team effectiveness, 19–21
Seduction of the Innocent, The (Wertham), 234
Seeds of Greatness, The (Waitley), 120
self-reflection, 194
Serenity Prayer, 44
Shadow, 41
Shakespeare, William, 5
Sharma, Robin, 7, 24, 35
SHAZAM mnemonic, 76, 221–222
Shuster, Joe, 200
Siegel, Jerry, 200
Silver Age of Comics, 234
Silverstein, Ray, 161
Silver Surfer, the, 92–96
Simmons, Gene, 15
Simon, Joe, 143
simplicity, 194
Simpsons, The, 64
Sin City, 34
Sinestro, 188–195
Sinestro Corps War, The, 188
Singer, Jonathan, 70
Sony, 36
Spawn, 61–65
Spawn #1, 64
Spider-Man, 122–129
Star Wars, 133
Steinem, Gloria, 103
Stevenson, Robert Louis, 97
Steve Rogers, 144, 145
Stone, Oliver, 3
Stormwatch, 174
Strange Adventures #205, 57
Strange Case of Dr. Jekyll and Mr. Hyde, The (Stevenson), 97
Student magazine, 55

Sue Storm, 157, 159–160
Superboy and the Legion of Super-Heroes, 169
Superboy Starring the Legion of Super-Heroes, 169
Superman, 66–70
Surfing with the Alien (Satriani), 94
Surowiecki, James, 171, 172
SWIPE. *See* modeling

T

Tales of Penance, 231
Tales of Suspense #39, 117
Tales of the Teen Titans #44, 72
team members, 159–164, 229
  finders, minders, grinders, and binders, 160, 161–162
  roles of, knowing, 162–164
team-ups, being ready for, 25–30
  avoiding, 26–27
  importance of, 27–29
  making the most of, 29–30
  popularity of, 26
  structure of, 26
teamwork, 134–138, 228
  life as a team sport, 136–137
  role players, 137–138
Teen Titans, 72, 169
Ten Golden Rules, 3–37, 223
  be ready for team-ups, 25–30
  craft an identity, 15–19
  do no evil, 3–6
  establish a hideout, 22–23
  establish your MO, 13–15
  keep odd hours, 24–25
  keep your secrets, 19–22
  overcome adversity, 34–37
  patrol often network, 31–34
  swear an oath, 6–13
Thing, The, 159, 162
think before you act, 61–65, 226
  be careful what you wish for, 64–65
  karma, 63–64
Thor, 84–87
three Cs, avoiding, 126–129
300, 34
Time, 179
Tony Stark, 117, 118, 119, 120
Trump, Donald, 15
Turillo, Michael J., 162–163

U

"'Unsiloing' of Organizations, The," 186

V

value proposition, 11
Ventura, Jesse, 90
Venture Capital Breakfast Series, 33
Victoria's Secret, 167
Virgin Atlantic, 55
Virgin Galactic, 55
Virgin Records, 55
vision, 193
visualization, 49, 177–178

W

Waid, Mark, 235
Waitley, Dennis, 120
Wall Street, 3
Wal-Mart, 167
Walton, Sam, 167–168
Washington, Denzel, 173
Watchmen series, 77
weaknesses
  keeping your guard up, 66–70
  knowing, 69–70
Weapon X, 145
We Got Fired! . . . And It's the Best Thing That Ever Happened to Us (MacKay), 90–91
Wein, Len, 113
Welch, Jack, 115–116, 121, 146, 155
Welch, Suzy, 121
Wellesley College, 37
Wertham, Frederic, 234
West, Roland, 41
Whitehorn, William, 55
willpower (the will and the way), 47–56, 225
  authority, 54–56
  burnout, 54
  fears, 50–52
  "Law of Attraction," 49–50, 60
  visualization, power of, 49
  wisdom and, 52–53
Winfrey, Oprah, 37, 51, 73–74, 79
Winning: The Answers: Confronting 74 of the Toughest Questions in Business Today (Welch and Welch), 121
Wisdom of Crowds, The (Surowiecki), 171, 172
Wise, Bev, 125, 218
Wise Mentor Capital, 13, 104
Wise Words: Lessons in Entrepreneurship & Venture Capital (Wise), 33
Wizard: The Guide to Comics, 200
Wolverine, 113–116
Wonder Woman, 101–104
Woolworth, F. W., 37
Wu, Brian, 203–204

X

Xavier, Charles, 197, 199
X-Men, 30, 169, 196–197, 211

Z

zealot, 198
zealotry, 196–199, 229
Zipf's law, 114–115
Zorro, 41

PHOTO BY STEPHANIE LAKE PHOTOGRAPHY

ABOUT THE AUTHOR

Sean Wise is a true Business Superhero. His current roles include:

- Professor of Entrepreneurship at the Ted Rogers School of Business
- Industry adviser and online host of *Dragons' Den*, a business reality show about venture capital
- National entrepreneurship columnist for the *Toronto Globe and Mail*
- Founding partner at the New York–based venture capital firm Spencer Trask Collaborative Venture Partners
- Professor of entrepreneurship at Ryerson University in Toronto

Sean studied engineering and economics at Carleton University, received his law and MBA degrees from the University of Ottawa, and is now pursuing his PhD in business at the University of Glasgow in the United Kingdom.

Sean lives with his fiancée, Allison Hughes, and her cat, Strutter. He splits his time among his office in Manhattan, his home in Toronto, and his cottage by Lake Simcoe.